The Obscenity Report

The Obscenity Report

THE REPORT TO THE TASK FORCE
ON PORNOGRAPHY AND OBSCENITY

081920

Distributed by STEIN AND DAY/*Publishers*/New York

First published in 1970
Copyright © 1970 Stein and Day, Incorporated
Library of Congress Catalog Card No. 70-127235
All rights reserved
Published simultaneously in Canada by Saunders of Toronto Ltd.
Printed in the United States of America
Designed by Bernard Schleifer
Stein and Day/*Publishers*/7 East 48 Street, New York, N.Y. 10017
SBN 8128-1328-6

CONTENTS

PART I: A SEARCH FOR THE OBSCENE

PART II: A PROFILE:
AMERICA SILHOUETTED AGAINST OBSCENITY

PART III: THE CONTROL OF OBSCENITY

PART IV: RECOMMENDATIONS

June 1, 1970

The President
The White House

Dear Mr. President:

We are honored to forward this Report on Obscenity and Pornography.

Shortly after your inauguration, you indicated your desire for a Report on Obscenity and Pornography as soon and as comprehensive as possible to enable prompt formulation of a Presidential anti-obscenity program.

Consequently, the enclosed Report was prepared following around-the-clock efforts. Although it will be supplemented by several addenda before its official release to the public, this Report is in no sense an "interim" study. The recommendations contained herein are unanimously submitted after lengthy deliberations; the final Report will not in any significant degree deviate from this Report.

We understand, of course, that the enclosed Report is "interim" in the sense that it will not be released to the public. Nor shall our "final" Report refer to the enclosed study in any way. The confidentiality of this Report has thus permitted the utmost candor on our part.

We share your sense of urgency concerning the problems of obscenity, and we hope that this Report will be of assistance to you.

Respectfully yours,

/s/

PART I

A SEARCH FOR THE OBSCENE

Section 1: Toward a Realistic Definition of Obscenity and Pornography

A WIDELY QUOTED sentiment of a Justice of the United States Supreme Court has it that "hard-core pornography" can "perhaps" never successfully be "intelligently defined." [1] The attitude is not, for all its curious intellectual appeal, a new one, and it has worked unnecessary harm on civic-minded attempts at controlling the vicious outpouring of truly strong obscenity in recent years.

Some have said that defining obscenity is about as easy as catching fog in a net and about as necessary. Others have felt differently. Indeed, the late and distinguished Justice of the Supreme Court of Pennsylvania, Michael A. Musmanno, once lamented: "I cannot understand why a ponderous problem is made of definition of words. Obscenity—how can anyone doubt what it means? And yet [the courts] go into fine legal argumentation as to what it includes, and so on." [2] Likewise, the Chairman of the Philadelphia Citizens Committee Against Obscenity, Mrs. Walter A. Craig, has noted that "the old cliché that it is almost impossible to define obscenity leaves [the public] pretty cold—as it should. If we can define everything else under the sun in a workable

---

1. *Jacobellis v. Ohio*, 378 U.S. 184, 197 (1964).
2. Testimony before the Subcommittee on Postal Operations of the Committee on Post Office and Civil Service, House of Representatives, 87th Congress, 1st Session, 1962. Printed in Hearings, *Obscene Matter Sent Through the Mail* [hereinafter, Hearings], p. 38.

definition, it is a little difficult to see why obscenity should be the exception." [3]

The fact of the matter is that even the courts have recognized that obscenity is not, in the words of Justice Holmes, some "brooding omnipresence in the sky." [4] It is, rather, a practical problem for practical people to resolve.

Fundamental to any attempt at controlling undesirable behavior is the definition of the behavior to be controlled. We have proceeded in two ways toward this end. First, we undertook to discover how various eminent sources have defined the pornographic. Since the obscene depends in large part on community acceptance or rejection, it was necessary, we thought, to see what members of the community in fact had to say about it. Second, we undertook to find actual examples of pornography, hoping to distill from these original sources the quintessence of the obscene. The definitions and the illustrations thus will help clarify one another.

Definitions of the obscene fall into two broad categories: those which view obscenity as matter which "disgusts," and those which view obscenity as matter which "excites lust" (what the courts have called "appealing to prurient interest"). These two categories are not so necessarily mutually contradictory as they might seem.

Both lay and legal lexicographers have tried their hands at defining obscenity.

The Random House Dictionary crystallizes the lay concept of obscenity: (1) "offensive to modesty or decency; indecent; lewd"; (2) "causing or tending to cause, sexual excitement or lust"; or (3) "abominable; disgusting; repulsive." The first aspect of the definition is obvious enough on its face; it means, quite simply, that the obscene is what would cause the average young man or woman on the street to blush. The illustration immediately following makes this point perfectly clear.

3. Hearings, p. 122.
4. Holmes, J., dissenting, in *Southern Pacific Co. v. Jensen*, 244 U.S. 205, 222 (1917).

"OFFENSIVE TO MODESTY . . . LEWD"

. . . because he doesnt know what it is to have one yes when I lit the lamp yes because he must have come 3 or 4 times with that tremendous big red brute of a thing he has I thought the vein or whatever the dickens they call it was going to burst though his nose is not so big after I took off all my things with the blinds down after my hours dressing and perfuming and combing it like iron or some kind of a thick crowbar standing all the time he must have eaten oysters I think a few dozen he was in great singing voice no I never in all my life felt anyone had one the size of that to make you feel full up he must have eaten a whole sheep after whats the idea making us like that with a big hole in the middle of us like a stallion driving it up into you because thats all they want out of you with that determined vicious look in his eye I had to halfshut my eyes still he hasnt such a tremendous amount of spunk in him when I made him pull it out and do it on me considering how big it is so much the better in case any of it wasnt washed out properly the last time I let him finish it in me. . . . (James Joyce, *Ulysses*, p. 742. New York: Modern Library, 1961)

The second aspect of the dictionary definition is more difficult to illustrate, since one man's lust is another man's filth, and thus it may strike some that illustrations of the second aspect are more appropriately illustrations of the third. While we do not, therefore, make any pretense that the second illustration has been scientifically determined to represent the second aspect, it is close enough.

"CAUSING . . . LUST"

"You're a slave driver," Carmella said huskily, pressing the nipple of one massive breast into his arm. "I didn't think you were ever going to stop."

Richey reached over to a table nearby for a couple of drinks. When he handed her one, he let his eyes roam over her figure. . . .

She pressed closer to him, and desire rose in him quickly, now that the pressure and tension of the afternoon shooting sessions was over.

"I know you could use me," she said, her voice husky with passion that matched his. "And I like to be used."

Her body touched his, becoming more and more intimate as she moved against him skillfully, backing him against a wall. Then she melted her body into his, grinding her hips against him in an agony of desire.

"There are lots of ways to use a woman," he whispered huskily, blowing softly in her ear. "We've only used you one way."

. . . Carmella met him at the couch, tugging at his clothes in a frantic effort to undress him so that the awful longing within her would be filled. Then they knew nothing for several minutes but the fiery pounding of passion as they writhed together, locking frantically in a lust-filled embrace where each sought erotic stimulation from the other.

. . . She revelled in the masculinity of Richey White as she finally spread herself to receive him, clamping him to her in a desperate attempt to get every bit of passionate ecstasy he offered (Del Brit, *The Hard Sell Girls*, pp. 6, 7. After Hours, 1964)

The third aspect of the definition is itself in three parts: The obscene is that which is "abominable" or "disgusting" or "repulsive." Again, these aspects may be illustrated with passages from pornographic literature which we gleaned— and which any ordinary American citizen might glean— from the shelves of a local bookstore.

"ABOMINABLE; DISGUSTING; REPULSIVE"

"Th'art good cunt, though, aren't ter? Best bit o'cunt left on earth. When ter likes! When tha'rt willin'!"

"What is cunt?" she asked.

"An' doesn't ter know? Cunt! It's thee down theer; an' what I get when I'm i'side thee; it's a' as it is, all on't."

"All on't," she teased. "Cunt! It's like fuck then."

"Nay, nay! Fuck's only what you do. Animals fuck. But cunt's a lot more than that. It's thee, dost see: an' tha'rt a lot besides an animal, aren't ter? even ter fuck! Cunt! Eh, that's the beauty o' thee, lass." (D. H. Lawrence, *Lady Chatterley's Lover*, pp. 233–234. New York: Grove Press, 1962)

It should be evident at this point that the definitional problem is not beyond solution. Indeed, the dictionaries have done it handily.[5] For as Huntington Cairns aptly said more than thirty years ago: "There is no difficulty in distinguishing between books the impulse behind which is literary and those whose impulse is pornography. Any man with a modicum of literary knowledge can do so without hesitation." [6] It should not pass without noting that the late Mr. Zechariah Chafee, an outstanding constitutional authority, professor at Harvard Law School, and long-time defender of free speech, himself described Mr. Cairns as "the ideal censor." [7]

To these considerations must now be added the tests established by the courts of the United States. Discussions of obscenity are neither complete nor relevant without recourse to legal standards, because so much of the long drama of modern obscenity has been played in the courtroom. Though we shall delve more thoroughly into a consideration of the legal tests in a later section of this Report,[8] a statement of them is not out of place here. They should be firmly fixed in mind.

The Supreme Court, in its most recent pronouncement, has stated that to be legally obscene "three elements must coalesce: It must be established that (a) the dominant theme of the material taken as a whole appeals to a prurient

5. *Webster's Third New International Dictionary* (unabridged) defines obscene thus: "1*a*: disgusting to the senses usually because of some filthy, grotesque, or unnatural quality; *b*: grossly repugnant to the generally accepted notions of what is appropriate: shocking; 2: offensive or revolting as countering or violating some ideal or principle: as *a*: abhorrent to morality or virtue: stressing or reveling in the lewd or lustful; specifically: inciting or designed to incite to lust, depravity or indecency; *b*: marked by violation of accepted language inhibitions and by the use of words regarded as taboo in polite usage; *c*: repulsive by reason of malignance, hypocrisy, cynicism, irresponsibility, crass disregard of moral or ethical principles." The Webster definition thus coincides in spirit, if not in letter, with that of the *Random House Dictionary*.

6. From "Freedom of Expression in Literature," *1938 Annals of the American Academy of Political and Social Science*, 87.

7. In *Government and Mass Communications*, I (Chicago: University of Chicago Press, 1947), p. 269.

8. See p. 84.

interest in sex; (b) the material is patently offensive because it affronts contemporary community standards relating to the description or representation of sexual matters; and (c) the material is utterly without redeeming social value." [9] In this regard it should also be noted that the prurient-appeal requirement is "to be assessed in terms of the sexual interests of its intended and probable recipient group." [10]

The language of the Court, though forbidding to the untutored eye, means, in fact, nothing more or less than the definitions the dictionaries have already given. If the material appeals to a prurient interest, that is, if it tends to cause sexual excitement or lust; if it affronts contemporary standards, that is, if it is offensive to modesty or decency; and if it is utterly without redeeming social value, that is, if it is abominable, disgusting, or repulsive—it is obscene, and may properly be reached under existing legislation. Moreover, examples of the abominable, disgusting, and repulsive turn out to be passages devoid of redeeming social value.

"ABOMINABLE"

At night when I look at Boris' goatee lying on the pillow I get hysterical. O Tania, where now is that warm cunt of yours, those fat, heavy garters, those soft, bulging thighs? There is a bone in my prick six inches long. I will ream out every wrinkle in your cunt, Tania, big with seed. I will send you home to your Sylvester with an ache in your belly and your womb turned inside out. Your Sylvester! Yes, he knows how to build a fire, but I know how to inflame a cunt. I shoot hot bolts into you, Tania, I make your ovaries incandescent. Your Sylvester is a little jealous now? He feels something, does he? He feels the remnants of my big prick. I have set the shores a little wider, I have ironed out the wrinkles. After me you can take on stallions, bulls, rams, drakes, St. Bernards. You can stuff toads, bats, lizards up your rectum. You can shit arpeggios if you like, or string

9. *John Cleland's Memoirs of a Woman of Pleasure v. Attorney General of Massachusetts*, 383 U.S. 413, 418 (1966).
10. *Mishkin v. New York*, 383 U.S. 502, 509 (1966).

a zither across your navel. I am fucking you, Tania, so that you'll stay fucked. And if you are afraid of being fucked publicly I will fuck you privately. I will tear off a few hairs from your cunt and paste them on Boris' chin. I will bite into your clitoris and spit out two franc pieces. . . . (Henry Miller, *The Tropic of Cancer,* pp. 5–6. New York: Grove Press, 1961)

"DISGUSTING"

Down there, she felt a quick new tremor. Her lips parted. Dick smiled. "You feel something?" he said. Dottie nodded. "You'd like it again?" he said, assaying her with his hand. Dottie stiffened; she pressed her thighs together. She was ashamed of the violent sensation his exploring fingers had discovered. But he held his hand there, between her clasped thighs, and grasped her right hand in his other, guiding it . . . over that part of himself, which was soft and limp, rather sweet, really, all curled up on itself like a fat worm. Sitting beside her, he looked into her face as he stroked her down there and tightened her hand on him. "There's a little ridge there," he whispered. "Run your fingers up and down it." Dottie obeyed, wonderingly; she felt his organ stiffen a little, which gave her a strange sense of power. (Mary McCarthy, *The Group,* p. 44, Signet, New York, 1964)

"REPULSIVE"

When she raised the belt again it was obvious she would flog me if I did not obey. Then she said, "You're unprotected —naked—a naked slave! And I can do what I want with you —even ruin your manhood."

A pang of fear tore into my heart. I could feel the loud thumping. She was right. I was helpless—and she had me in her power. It was frightening—but so stimulating! Woodenly, I dropped to my hands and knees and waited her next order. . . . I screamed from the lightning pain that streaked across my back. "Don't." I was sobbing. "Don't . . . whip me!"

"I like to see the way your body jerks and spasms when I whip you—so obey my orders or I'll flog you until you're groveling at my feet."

. . . As for myself, the way she kept digging the heel of the flying foot into where it really hurt me the most was also a spear of passion. . . . "Remove my panties," she gasped. "Hurry! HURRY!" . . . The still moist stockings and damp panties made a silky bundle in my palms. Humbly I looked up at her, ever conscious of the bullwhip-like belt in her hand and my naked condition. "Bury your face in that—and kiss them!" I felt a whirring noise. Everything was spinning. But I obeyed and kissed the soft, warm and moist panties and stockings. . . . "Quick," she ordered. "Take off my dress." She stood up. . . . She was a dream!! A living dream! Her body was milky white. The twin headlights—and they were as big as enormous searchlights—shook like twin vats of jelly. The red globs on the tips became larger and larger. . . . When I reached her milky white thighs, the fragrance of sandalwood and myrrh assailed my nostrils. I tangled in the forbidden grotto of Aphrodite, peered down the treacherous but so desirable valley of Eve—and suddenly, I did something I would never have done before. . . . (Robert Justin, *Hot Lips,* pp. 100, 101–102, 103, 104, 105. Branden House, 1964)

The problem, as we shall see, is that the courts seem equivocal in applying this definition. It will be no surprise to officials who have long been concerned about the problems of obscenity that of the books excerpted above, many have been declared under current or earlier legal tests not to be obscene. In part, this has to do with the First Amendment to the Federal Constitution, which we shall consider in a later section. But the gist of many judicial decisions is that what is obscene may not be obscene, an obviously paradoxical result that lends only confusion to an area where clarity is much to be preferred.[11]

11. At the same time, it is pertinent to note here that the courts have not—as some extreme critics of the courts contend—permitted *all* pornography to flourish openly. The Supreme Court itself, as recently as 1966, declared more than fifty books to be obscene and not protected by the First Amendment:

1. *Chances Go Around*
2. *Impact*
3. *Female Sultan*
4. *Satin Satellite*
5. *Her Highness*
6. *Mistress of Leather*
7. *Educating Edna*
8. *Strange Passions*
9. *The Whipping Chorus Girls*
10. *Order of the Day*

The foregoing definitions, therefore, are clearly a realistic means by which to classify and categorize the obscene and the pornographic. For it remains but to subject the putatively pornographic to this analysis: (1) Is it offensive? (2) Does it incite to lust? (3) Is it repulsive and without redeeming value? These tests are easy to state and should be no more difficult to apply. For as Justice Stewart has said of the pornographic: "I know it when I see it." [12]

OBSCENITY AS PSYCHOLOGICAL DISINTEGRATION

It is worth stressing that the critical element of obscenity is its tendency to corrupt, deprave, or incite. If pornography did no more to anyone than do the poems of Lord Tennyson, there would be neither cause for alarm nor need for definition. But as Professor William E. Hocking, of the phil-

---

11. *Bound Martially*
12. *Dance with the Dominant Whip*
13. *Cult of the Spankers*
14. *Confessions*
15. *The Hours of Torture*
16. *Bound in Rubber*
17. *Arduous Figure Training at Bondhaven*
18. *Return Visit to Fetterland*
19. *Fearful Ordeal in Restraintland*
20. *Women in Distress*
21. *Pleasure Parade No. 1*
22. *Screaming Flesh*
23. *Fury*
24. *So Firm So Fully Packed*
25. *I'll Try Anything Twice*
26. *Masque*
27. *Catanis*
28. *The Violated Wrestler*
29. *Betrayal*
30. *Swish Bottom*

31. *Raw Dames*
32. *The Strap Returns*
33. *Dangerous Years*
34. *Columns of Agony*
35. *The Tainted Pleasure*
36. *Intense Desire*
37. *Pleasure Parade No. 4*
38. *Pleasure Parade No. 3*
39. *Pleasure Parade No. 2*
40. *Sorority Girls Stringent Initiation*
41. *Terror at the Bizarre Museum*
42. *Temptation*
43. *Peggy's Distress on Planet Venus*
44. *Ways of Discipline*
45. *Mrs. Tyrant's Finishing School*
46. *Perilous Assignment*
47. *Bondage Correspondence*
48. *Women Impelled*
49. *Eye Witness*
50. *Stud Broad*
51. *Queen Bee*

Books cited in *Mishkin v. New York*, 383 U.S. 502, 514 (1966). This list is not atypical of the many which are compiled daily by law enforcement officers. As Louis Slaton, district attorney of Fulton County, Georgia, has noted of the list of hundreds of obscene books he has compiled: "The list is probably as obscene as anything they're selling." Quoted in *The New York Times*, September 15, 1969.

12. *Jacobellis v. Ohio*, 378 U.S. 184, 197 (1964).

osophy department at Harvard University, said as long ago
as 1947:

> A published obscenity is not an idle mental image—it is a
> disruptive mental image, a violent displacement of the self-
> sense of the viewer from the region of active purpose to the
> region of bodily preoccupation; it intrudes upon the eye
> what is normally in the province of touch and concealment;
> it begins a psychological disintegration.[13]

This disintegration is startlingly apparent in the next
passage.

"DISINTEGRATION"

On the occasion of a "high congress" the Mrigi (Deer)
woman should lie down in such a way as to widen her yoni,
while in a "low congress" the Hastini (Elephant) woman
should lie down so as to contract hers. But in an "equal congress" they should lie down in the natural position. What is
said above concerning the Mrigi and the Hastini applies also
to the Vadawa (Mare) woman. In a "low congress" the
woman should particularly make use of medicine, to cause
her desires to be satisfied quickly.

The Deer-woman has the following three ways of lying
down:

> The widely opened position
> The yawning position
> The position of the wife of Indra

When she lowers her head and raises her middle parts, it
is called the "widely opened position." At such a time the
man should apply some unguent, so as to make the entrance
easy. (*The Kama Sutra of Vatsyayana*, p. 120. New York:
Capricorn, 1963)

As Robert W. Edwards, Deputy Collector of Customs,
U.S. Customs Mail Division, Boston, has said, the *Kama
Sutra* "bears the dubious distinction of being the filthiest

13. In *Freedom of the Press* (Chicago: University of Chicago
Press, 1947), p. 122.

book published today [1962]. . . . In my opinion, the human mind is scarcely able to withstand the impact of the overwhelming obscenity and sexually based desire for torture [in] the *Kama Sutra*." [14]

The Tokyo High Court itself has observed that "obscene literature is literature which excites or stirs up sexual organs or sexual behavior, spoils normal sexual modesty and is contrary to good sexual morals." [15] And the American Law Institute's Model Penal Code has in the past defined obscenity as follows: "A thing is obscene if, considered as a whole, its predominant appeal is to prurient interest, *i.e.*, a shameful or morbid interest in nudity, sex, or excretion, and if it goes substantially beyond customary limits of candor in description or representation of such matters." [16]

DISGUST VERSUS TITILLATION

Some people have remarked on the contradiction between defining obscenity as that which excites and defining it as that which disgusts; they suggest that if it excites it doesn't disgust and if it disgusts it cannot excite.[17] Though, properly speaking, these are psychological questions that cannot appropriately be considered in the definitional section of this Report, a way out of this seeming paradox is easily supplied here. For we do not suggest that obscenity is either one *or* the other. We suggest that obscenity is *both*.

14. Hearings, p. 238.
15. May 10, 1951; quoted in Terence J. Murphy, *Censorship: Government and Obscenity* (Baltimore: Helicon Press, 1963), p. 34.
16. ALI, Model Penal Code, Section 207.10(2) (Tent. Draft No. 6, 1957).
17. See, for example, Willard M. Gaylin, "The Prickly Problems of Pornography," 77 *Yale Law Journal* 479 (1968).

NOT ALL EXPRESSIONS OF SEX ARE WRONG

It is obviously too late in the day to go about suggesting, as some might, that any reference to sex is indecent and there-fore wrong. We live in an advanced society, and a complex and interdependent one; technological requirements and social imperatives are not to be met by denying sex. Sex exists.[18]

Rather, the problem is to distinguish—as the above-cited definitions clearly do—between right and wrong uses of sex. The point can be made clearer by exploring an actual court case that arose in Oklahoma in 1953. A Negro man was discovered by police officers to be fondling the right breast of a white woman and kissing her on the nape of the neck as she lay on a desk in her husband's law office.[19] Both were drunk. The woman had been involved with the man before. This time the man was charged with and convicted of an act of lewdness and sentenced to a year in jail. At the appeal to the Oklahoma Supreme Court, the man's defense counsel argued that the acts in which he had engaged were not lewd. But the learned court knocked counsel's argument into a cocked hat, saying:

> Two persons meeting and kissing or lovers arm in arm and petting but showing high respect each for the other is one thing, and sensual acts as shown by the evidence in the within case is another. The first illustration may be elevat-ing, while the latter is definitely degrading, and even as ad-mitted by counsel, nauseating. The position of the woman on the desk and the acts of the defendant could only be calcu-lated to arouse the sensual and lustful passion of the parties,

18. There is, of course, another reason to admit its existence. To do otherwise would be to create a serious credibility gap which might serve to make the federal campaign against obscenity, in the words of one of our members, "another God-damned Haynsworth."

19. The court conceded that the charges, which denoted that the man was black and the woman white, were improper; accordingly the court reduced the sentence of the man from one year to six months. The woman was not charged.

and the compelling presumption is that the conduct was the natural prelude to forthcoming sexual relations that was only interrupted by the appearance of the officers.[20]

The distinction is apparent: Sexual relations, when the lovers have high regard for one another, are entirely permissible and, hence, definitely not capable of possessing the quality of lewdness, so long as the sensual and lustful passions are removed. The court is to be understood in its broadest sense, and the mere fact that the incipient relationship would presumably have been adulterous or that the woman was indecorously spread on a desk was not the sum and substance of the court's holding. Even D. H. Lawrence, author of *Lady Chatterley's Lover,* has advocated sanctions against the cheap trivialization of sex: "Literature [he said] which debases sex should be censored." [21]

THE MARTIAN OBSERVER

Now and again it has been suggested [22] that were a man from Mars to come to earth, and specifically to the United States, he would be quite astonished at the elaborate lengths to which we sometimes go to surround the sexual aspect of the body in myth and mystery. The suggestion goes that while we would be greatly shocked if some of our more popular men and women were suddenly to cast aside their clothing and walk along the streets of our major metropolises utterly naked, or pose thus on television before millions of Americans, the Martian would naturally find it quite curious that we would be so shocked by the simple display of our biological selves. What, he would ask, is so disgusting about our God-given bodies?

20. *Landrum v. State,* 255 P.2d 525, 531 (Crim. Ct. App. Okla. 1953).
21. D. H. Lawrence, "Pornography and Censorship," in *Sex, Literature, and Censorship,* Harry T. Moore ed. (New York: Twayne, 1953).
22. See, for example, Hearings, pp. 279 ff.

There is nothing disgusting about the *body in itself.* And if that were all that it were a matter of, we would agree with the Martian that the whole matter is somewhat curious. But, as later sections of this Report indicate, it is not simply the *body in itself* with which we must contend. We must concern ourselves with the *body in context:* the attitudes and suggestions and symbols which surround the body in undress or in motion or the description of men and women engaged in erotic play. This is a cultural phenomenon which would be so foreign to the Martian that he would mistake it altogether for false modesty, mere prudery, or downright priggishness. It is this important cultural context which critics so often miss and which so often makes us think that there may be Martians on the courts, given the misunderstandings and mistakes in our federal jurisprudence. Pornography is not merely a state of mind, it is a state of action. Thus the context is important.

Section 2: Types of Obscenity

WITH AN UNDERSTANDING of the meaning of obscenity behind us, it is not difficult to spot the different kinds of obscenity that flourish openly in society today.

BOOKS AND MANUSCRIPTS

With one type of obscenity—literary pornography—everyone is familiar. This has been one of the most ancient forms of obscene expression. Manuscripts of pornographic stories have circulated in one form or another since the invention of writing itself. The illustrations contained in the review of definitions indicate the range of pornographic literature.

Even the most famous and artistic of literary men have from time to time succumbed to the temptation to turn out a pornographic work. Mark Twain, for instance, who turned out children's classics still read by students today, penned one of the most notorious works of pornography of all time —*1601*, a supposed dialogue between Queen Elizabeth I and her royal court, including Sir Walter Raleigh. It is a work that is unequaled in the vileness of its obscenity. Indeed, as long ago as the turn of the century, it gained reputation enough for the Secretary of State, John Hay, to have a limited edition secretly printed on the presses at the United

States Military Academy at West Point.[1] There is no indication, however, that any of these copies have ever fallen into the wrong hands.

For sheer quantity and ease of transmission, the printed word in the form of book or manuscript is probably the single greatest source of obscenity in the modern world.

FILMS AND PLAYS

Until recently, the dramatic work and the motion picture were not sources of pornography. For one thing, the very public quality of the live dramatic work or the cinematic presentation made any pornographic content thereof easily detectable. For another, it is reasonably easy for a person without scruples to write out a pornographic novel for quick and anonymous publication and circulation, but a play or movie makes it far more likely that the actor will be apprehended. Finally, most people will commit obscenity to paper more unblushingly than they would perform it, so for a time plays and movies were necessarily self-policing. And of course, insofar as the film was a new medium, subject to the discipline of self-regulation, untoward sexual references could be minimized.

Of course, there have always been women who would strip for money, just as there have always been prostitutes. So, as the new immorality developed, actors and actresses lost their reticence, and the result today is unabashed nudity and obscene language in play after play, movie after movie, even in the so-called legitimate theater, as the following illustration makes clear.

BOY: When I come it's like a river. It's all over the bed and
   the sheets and everything. You know? I mean a short
   vagina gives me security. I can't help it. I like to feel
   like I'm really turning a girl on. It's a much better

1. Morris L. Ernst and Alan U. Schwartz, *Censorship: The Search for the Obscene* (New York: Macmillan, 1964), p. 36.

screw is what it amounts to. I mean if a girl has a really small vagina it's really better to go in from behind. You know? I mean she can sit with her legs together and you can sit facing her. You know? But that's different. It's just a different kind of thing. You can do it standing, you know? Just by backing her up, you know? You just stand and she goes down and down until she's almost sitting on your dick. You know what I mean? She'll come a hundred times and you just stand there holding onto it. That way you don't even have to undress. You know? I mean she may not even want to undress at all. I like to undress myself but some girls just don't want to. I like going down on girls too. You know what I mean? She gives me some head and then I give her some. Just sort of a give and take thing. You know? The thing with a big vagina is that there isn't as much contact. There isn't as much friction. I mean you can move around inside her. There's different ways of ejaculation. I mean the leading up to it can be different. You can rotate motions. Actually girls really like fingers almost as well as a penis. . . . (*Oh! Calcutta!*, p. 102. New York: Grove Press, 1969)

There has been for many years a more serious problem with reference to "stag" or "skin" movies. These are unashamedly obscene movies made by nonestablished cameramen purely for profit on low budgets. That they have long flourished is a well-known fact; most members of college fraternities can attest to having seen one at some time or another. But the interstate aspect of obscene movies has greatly expanded in recent years. Recently in the news, for instance, was the arrest of Judge Edward A. Haggerty, of New Orleans, for conspiring to commit obscenity, among other charges.[2] He was alleged to have been attending a "before-the-wedding bachelor's party" at which "stag movies" were shown. The judge had presided over the Clay Shaw–Kennedy conspiracy trial. Thus, today, even reputable people are becoming involved in this type of obscenity.

2. See *The Washington Post*, December 19, 1969, p. A3.

THE SPOKEN WORD: PROFANITY

The spoken word itself is a very serious source of obscenity throughout the United States. It is not at all amiss to note the words of the President of the United States when he was a candidate for that office in 1960. Speaking of former President Truman's proclivity to use rough language in public, then Vice President Richard M. Nixon said during the third television debate:

When a man is President of the United States or a former President, he has an obligation not to lose his temper in public. One thing I have noted as I have traveled around the country are the tremendous number of children who come out to see the presidential candidates. I see mothers holding their babies up so that they can see a man who might be President of the United States. I know Senator Kennedy sees them too. It makes you realize that whoever is President is going to be a man that all the children of America will either look up to or will look down to, and I can only say that I am very proud that President Eisenhower restored dignity and decency and, frankly, good language to the conduct of the Presidency of the United States.[3]

We share this view. We would go farther. We believe that all men in public office should help restore decent language. On this subject we must be candid. It is not unknown that policemen and other public servants use foul language from time to time. That they are goaded into it by obscenity-screaming youths and others does not entirely excuse the moral lapse. Foul language only spreads decay, as it begets more foul language. It is the raw stuff of obscenity itself.

We should make no mistake about the prevalence of profanity. It is easy enough to overlook because of "the curious

3. October 13, 1960; printed in *The Joint Appearances of Senator John F. Kennedy and Vice President Richard M. Nixon, Presidential Campaign of 1960*, Final Report of the Committee on Commerce of the United States Senate, Part III, 87th Congress, 1st Session, Report 994, 1961, p. 210.

double standard which we permit but seldom recognize—
the moral imperative which we impose upon the young and
ignore in the adult. The child, for example, may be adjudged
delinquent for habitual use of profanity. The adult curse
goes unnoticed and unpunished." [4] From our own experience, the members of this Task Force could cite innumer-
able examples of citizens using indecent language—public
office holders, business executives, laborers, athletes, and
even housewives, not to mention the young people of
America on whom the future of the nation depends. When
the Attorney General of the United States himself—the
chief law enforcer of the nation—uses the phrase "what the
hell" in an interview with a distinguished reporter of *The
New York Times* for public attribution,[5] it is clear that the
spoken word has become a type of obscenity.[6]

ART, PICTURES, AND MUSIC

Another common kind of pornography is that depicted in
art, pictures, and music. Everyone has seen flesh magazines

4. Harrison E. Salisbury, Book Review, *Understanding Juvenile
Delinquency*, by Lee R. Steiner, 70 *Yale Law Journal* 333 (1960).
5. *The New York Times*, December 21, 1969, p. 1.
6. And a popular type at that. Collations of comprehensive surveys
conducted in representative American cities showed the following
verbal tendencies toward obscenity:

		CITY SIZE OVER 1,000,000	500,000– 1,000,000	250,000– 500,000	100,000– 250,000	LESS THAN 100,000
Percent of fre- quency in total	pshaw	insig- nificant	0.1%	0.1%	0.3%	0.4%
verbiage of	fart	0.1%	0.1	0.2	0.2	0.3
specified word in	shit	0.2	0.2	0.3	0.3	0.2
ascending order of	fuck	0.5	0.4	0.3	0.2	0.1
verbal grossness	prick	0.2	0.2	0.1	insig- nificant	insig- nificant

The chart illustrates the puritan schism among our big-city people.
Even in large cities, where grossness indices suggest a more exag-
gerated level of verbal obscenity, the highest incidence of popular
grossness occurs only at the penultimate level of grossness. This
confirms the old saw, "No matter how dirty you get, you can always
get dirtier."

on the newsstands with scantily clad women (or men) on the cover and, presumably, undressed men and women on the inside. Though by statute in some states the degree of exposure is specifically circumscribed, these magazines with their color photographs circulate nonetheless. Texas is quite explicit that the line of pornography lies at the woman's breast "below the top of the nipple." [7] Without an opaque covering beyond that point, it is illegal to sell such a picture to youths under eighteen. Yet these magazines are regularly on sale at the newsstands of Texas.

Even more striking are the pictures, sketches, etchings, and paintings that hang in the major art galleries of the United States. There is no requirement that a person be above a certain age before he or she can enter an art gallery or museum, nor is there usually a requirement that a child be accompanied by a parent. Yet in galleries from Washington, D. C., to San Francisco, pictures of naked people are regularly displayed, and in Europe the situation is even more deplorable. Sometimes these pictures masquerade as culture—for example, the projected Kronhausen art tour through the United States of notorious erotic paintings from Europe. But a naked body is naked, whether it be in oil or in the flesh. The country should view with distress the disturbing tendency of religious greeting cards to expose areas of cherubim's bodies which are best left private.

Music is an area long neglected by students of obscenity and long exploited by smut slingers unfettered by legal sanctions. To remedy the situation, the Task Force subjected volunteer groups to countless varieties of sound. Because all evidence indicates that aural excitation does not vary significantly according to volume, the Task Force considered abandoning its tentative goal of classifying music as obscene according to decibel level.

However, objective standards for defining obscenity are difficult enough to come by without rejecting obvious ones. If the country is seriously interested in banning obscenity in music, a clear-cut criterion of permissible decibel levels,

7. Texas Penal Code, Article 534b, Section 3(b).

to be established by the Federal Communications Commission, would be sufficiently measurable to make even the most oversexed music maker or music lover chary.

ADVERTISING

A modern form of obscenity has been created by the advertising profession. In some respects, the sexy advertisement is the most insidious type of pornography because the reader, the watcher, and the listener do not always know directly how they are being exploited or debased. A recent article in *The Detroit News* [8] by Kathy McMeel makes the point clear beyond a doubt:

YOU DIRTY OLD AD MEN MAKE ME SICK

A love goddess runs down the beach, waves nibbling at her toes, her blond streaked hair sweeping back behind wide, expectant eyes. A flimsy garment clings to every supple curve. She runs faster, arms open, until finally she throws herself breathlessly into HIS arms. . . .

Where's this scene? Right in your living room, that's where.

Wild and passionately aroused, she can't stop herself. She runs her fingers through his hair, knocks his glasses off and kisses him and kisses him again. . . .

What's watching? Your nine-year-old daughter as she sits on her stuffed panda bear and wipes jelly off her face?

Now a smoldering tigress herself lies on a tiger-skin rug, teasing, beckoning. Through wet, sensuous lips she purrs a dare: Are you man enough for her?

Is who man enough? Your goggly-eyed male offspring, twelve, who's waiting for "Land of the Giants" or "Gunsmoke" to come back on and who has only just begun to have faint notions of what this boy-girl stuff's all about? . . .

And even more serious than the overt sexuality in advertising is its ability to exploit the psychology of subliminal

8. Reprinted in *Advertising Age*, December 1, 1969, p. 28.

perception. For advertising can put across a message in exceedingly subtle ways. On television, an advertisement need not be overtly pornographic to carry the erotic message to the viewer. It can come on as a simple and apparently harmless presentation, but the results can be sociologically and psychologically damaging.[9]

To the general harms that advertising and other types of obscenity can wreak on an unsuspecting (and suspecting) society, we must now turn.

9. Advertising is not the only medium of obscenity distribution, of course. The following table (from 75 *Yale Law Journal* 1409–10 [1966]) indicates how many kinds of disseminators there are:

advertisement	instrument	picture book
article	language	play
ballad	leaflet	presentation
book	letter	print
booklet	literature	publication
card	lithograph	record
carving	machinery used	recording
cast	magazine	representation
circular	material	silhouette
comic book	matter	slide
composition	model	statue
cut	newspaper	story
daguerreotype	notice on prevention	story paper
dance	or cure of sexual	stereoscopic picture
description	or menstrual disease	substance
design	novelty device	thing
device	object	thing rejected
drawing	painting	by U.S. mails
embodiment	pamphlet	thing to procure
engraving	paper	abortion or prevent
equipment used	periodical	conception
figment	performance	transcription
figure	phonograph record	writing
film	photography	
image	picture	

In one state or another all these various types of dissemination have at one time or another been banned or prohibited when they have carried obscenity.

PART II

A PROFILE: AMERICA SILHOUETTED
AGAiNST OBSCENITY

Section 1: Should Obscenity Be Eliminated?

THE TASK FORCE recognizes the real fact that there are dissenters to the proposition that obscenity is an evil to be eliminated. In fairness, we have therefore endeavored to treat the subject on a *tabula rasa,* and to address ourselves to the basic question of whether or not obscenity should in fact be fought. It would, of course, be easy for the nation blithely to steel itself against obscenity without bringing to the issue any degree of empathy for and real understanding of the position espoused by a vocal segment of the American community. But this segment is not simply a "lunatic fringe"; rather, real people, Americans with rights, honestly share deep convictions that nothing is wrong with obscenity. The Task Force has therefore sought, with all the objectivity, impartiality, and integrity at our command, to address the basic questions: Should obscenity be eliminated? If so, why? If not, why not? The voice of dissent has a right to be heard in America; we have respected that right, even when we have not agreed with it; and we have considered the arguments of that voice before endorsing our ultimate positions.

Apologists for obscenity rely upon the stanchion of the First Amendment. They argue that the constitutional proscription against abridging freedom of speech envelops obscenity within its protection. The dangers of suppressing any form of expression, they urge, so far outweigh the potential dangers of the suppressed materials as to present risks out of proportion to supposed benefit.

Furthermore, argue the spokesmen for obscenity, the difficulties of drawing a line beyond which expression will not be tolerated are fraught with totalitarian perils. Where, and by whom, and for what purposes, is the line to be drawn? The ability to function without fear of having expression prohibited is the key to the lock of genius. In the words of one of their historical spokesmen:

> Without an element of the obscene there can be no true and deep aesthetic or moral conception of life. . . . It is only the great men who are truly obscene. If they had not dared to be obscene they could never have dared to be great.[1]

In short, they say, both the Constitution and the creative impulse sanctify obscenity.

Supporters of the legitimacy of obscenity center on a respectable, if small, intellectual community. For the most part, they include college professors, their students, and other academics, many based in New York City and Washington, D. C. No less ardent advocates of the same position are journalists and publishers throughout the country. They are joined, of course, by the actual purveyors of obscenity, but are not to be condemned for or classified by that association.

The Task Force recognizes that these people are earnest. They are solid citizens, and they have no less a right to advocate their viewpoint than we have to advocate ours. But to accept their right to argument is not to accept their argument. As advocates of the supremacy of expression, they are more vociferous in its defense than are its detractors. However, national policy on an issue of this magnitude cannot be resolved by a simple decibel count, but by reason. We do note, though, that a survey sponsored by the Task Force showed that, of all Americans asked "Do you think obscenity should be allowed?", 74 percent answered no, 7 percent had no opinion, and only 19 percent answered yes.

We do not suggest that that poll itself provides an an-

---

1. Havelock Ellis, *Impressions and Comments* (3d and final series) (Boston: Houghton Mifflin Co., 1924), pp. 199–200.

swer to the complex problem. It does, however, reflect the strong distaste of a majority, albeit a silent one, for the spread of obscenity. That is not a fact to be trifled with; in our present-day concern with the rights of individuals, we should not lose sight of the fact that we are, after all, a democracy, and our laws should reflect the will of the people.

But there are reasons beyond those of sheer numbers for rejecting the reasons advanced in support of obscenity and stripping from it the shield of legitimacy. Basically, its defense is only a one-issue stand. Certainly, it *is* difficult to draw the line separating impermissible from legitimate expression. But this country has proved its mettle in solving difficult tasks before, and is ably equipped to solve this one as well. Any nation with the ingenuity to send men to the moon is capable of drawing the line between obscenity and nonobscenity.

Nor is the Task Force able to accept the suggestion that obscenity is in some sense the key to genius. Some of man's, and America's, most significant products of ingenuity stem from enterprises far removed from the specter of obscenity: our space exploits, our computer systems, our transportation, our technology. Nowhere in these areas did the absence of obscenity quell progress.

Basically, the spokesmen for obscenity present a one-argument case. We do not mean to suggest that that argument is totally without redeeming value. We do suggest, however, that on balance the dangers of obscenity so totally eclipse its conceivable value as to militate for its demise. Nor do we imply even remotely the slightest curtailment of freedom of speech under the First Amendment. We simply conclude that the dangers posed by obscenity are so great that obscenity should be eliminated without violating in the slightest the guarantees of the First Amendment.[2]

In the final analysis, there is simply a plethora of reasons suggesting the wisdom of a ban on obscenity. Not the least of these is the demonstrable correlation between rising obscenity statistics and rising crime rates. We are well

2. See "The Limits of Censorship," Part III, Section 2 of this Report.

aware, of course, not only of the inherent factors of unreliability in all statistics, but also of their particular unreliability in the area of crime, where so much is unreported and where, across the nation, so many different reporting systems are used. Nevertheless, the Uniform Crime Reports of the Federal Bureau of Investigation (FBI), a collation of statistics provided by enforcement agencies throughout the country, do provide the most meaningful available picture of crime in America. The FBI figures suggest a rather telling picture of the relationship between increasing obscenity rates and concomitant increasing crime rates (see facing page).

We do not suggest that these figures prove beyond peradventure that crime generally rises because of rises in obscenity violations. The figures do suggest, however, a correlation which, at the least, does not disprove assertions by extremely responsible officials, very much concerned with the problem, that there is indeed a causal nexus between obscenity and crime generally. As J. Edgar Hoover, Director of the Federal Bureau of Investigation, has himself acknowledged, "Filthy literature . . . is creating criminals faster than jails can be built." [3] Indeed, Dr. Nicholas G. Frignito, Medical Director and Chief Neuropsychiatrist of the County Court of Philadelphia, has concluded in one major finding that 95 percent of all delinquent boys, and 75 percent of all delinquent girls, "are familiar with these playing cards that have indecent pictures on their reverse side." [4]

The proposition that obscenity breeds criminal misconduct finds support not only in common sense, but in scholarly writing by experts often highly regarded by those who favor acceptance of obscenity. Even in the absence of scientific demonstration, heightened desire for sexual gratification—whether or not at the price of assault, robbery, or theft—would seem clearly to produce heightened pressures for that gratification, whence the short step to satis-

3. Quoted in Brown and Buchanan, "We Learned What Pornography Really Is," *Liberty*, March–April, 1966, p. 9.
4. Hearings, p. 68.

Index Crime Trends, 1930–1970 [5]

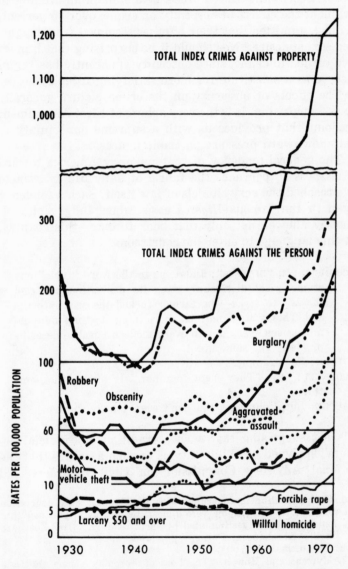

5. *Report of the President's Commission on Law Enforcement and Administration of Justice* [hereinafter, Crime Commission Report], 1967, pp. 22–23.

faction and crime. Of 1,846 rapists (now in prison) interviewed by the Task Force's field staff in an attempt to document the effects of obscenity on crime, over 85 percent, or 1,583, admitted that their offenses stemmed from heightened sexual desire.[6] Nor should it be surprising that hippies have turned to crime, since obscenity apparently has begun to serve as a substitute for more satisfying foreplay.[7]

The effects of obscenity on the crime picture generally are not surprising. It is the very sphere of First Amendment freedoms that provides us with a supreme opportunity to exert downward pressure on crime figures.

The general tendency of contemporary America toward lawlessness so pervades the fabric of daily life as even to have reached the very citadels of law itself. Such a tendency began in the famous *Ulysses* case, when Judge John M. Woolsey allowed not only that book to enter this country, but this language to enter the courtroom:

COUNSEL FOR "ULYSSES": Judge, as to the word "fuck," one etymological dictionary gives its derivation as from *facere*—to make—the farmer fucked the seed into the soil. This, your honor, has more integrity than a euphemism used every day in every modern novel to describe precisely the same event.

JUDGE: For example. . . .

COUNSEL: Oh—"They slept together." It means the same thing.

JUDGE: But, Counselor, that isn't even usually the truth.[8]

It is not surprising that such a tradition of "judicial decorum" spawned legal institutions of such a nature that the National Advisory Commission on Civil Disorders had

6. Such a finding is consistent with the Kronhausens' conclusion that readers of pornography were almost unanimous in stating "that they had been sexually stimulated by their reading." Drs. Eberhard and Phyllis Kronhausen, *Pornography and the Law*, p. 148 (New York: Ballantine, 1960).

7. Myrtens and Howell, "The Loss of Foreplay among the California Hippies," 1968 *Journal of Sociological Research* 26.

8. Quoted in Ernst and Schwartz, *Censorship: The Search for the Obscene, op. cit.*, pp. 94–95.

frankly to report that, in time of civil disturbance, "the massive influx of arrested persons resulted in serious deprivation of legal rights." [9] It is not the purpose of this report to refute those charges simply because they reflect poorly on institutions of the so-called Establishment. Rather, we note the phenomenon with chagrin, and suggest that it is in fact but one serious manifestation of the national malaise of lawlessness. It is high time that Americans learned both to appreciate their freedoms and to respect their restrictions. In the words of the Harvard commencement citation for the LL.B., we must acknowledge and respect "those wise restraints that make men free." Self-discipline is a virtue we need not be ashamed of. When we have the will and self-control to forbid ourselves the objects of desire—desire as strong as naked lust—we can be confident of our ability to grow as a civilization.

Historians often suggest that the measure of a civilization is in fact its ability to deal with and eliminate crime. What more cogent reason for eliminating obscenity? There are so many social deviations, after all, and so few we can curb; so many of the ills of our country are products of conditions difficult and costly to change. Obscenity can be eliminated: is there any better reason for its demise? We have tried diligently over the years to eliminate it: should all that effort, and all those expended resources, go for naught?

Obscenity exerts an even more subtle pressure on man's capacity to commit crime. The effects of smut do not stop at the viewer's eyes, but penetrate into his psyche. As Freud has himself observed:

> In telling me about their early youth, particularly before puberty, people who have afterward become very respectable have informed me of forbidden actions which they committed at that time. . . . [E]ventually I was led to make a more thorough study of such incidents by some glaring and more accessible cases in which the misdeeds were com-

9. *Report of the National Advisory Commission on Civil Disorders* [hereinafter, Civil Disorders Report], Bantam Ed., 1968, p. 340.

mitted while the patients were actually under my treatment, and were no longer so young. Analytic work then brought the surprising discovery that such deeds were done principally because they were forbidden, and because their execution was accompanied by mental relief for their doer. He was suffering from an oppressive feeling of guilt, of which he did not know the origin, and after he had committed a misdeed this oppression was mitigated. His sense of guilt was . . . attached to something.[10]

That the causal connection between obscenity and apparently unrelated criminal offenses is subtle renders that connection no less viable. Whether the consumer of obscenity commits a crime of violence immediately following his exposure to obscenity because of aroused libidinous urgings, or whether he commits a similar crime some time afterward because of complex psychic guilt reactions, the result is in each case identical: A victim, himself entitled to the rights of citizenship, suffers in consequence. Every drop of blood spilled, every tear of anguish shed, every piece of property misappropriated as a result of the spread of obscenity bespeaks more eloquently than mere logic the evils that obscenity leaves in its wake.[11]

Obviously, different people react to sexual stimuli in

10. Sigmund Freud, *Criminals from a Sense of Guilt* (1916), Vol. 14, *The Standard Edition of the Complete Psychological Works of Sigmund Freud*, James Strachey, ed. (Hogarth Press and Institute of Psychoanalysis, 1957), p. 332.

11. In fairness to the Commission's objective of exploring fully all conceivable defenses of obscenity, we feel constrained to note that some defenders and purveyors of obscenity actually claim that obscenity acts as a substitute for antisocial sexual conduct, rather than as a stimulus. See, for example, Earl F. Murphy, "The Value of Pornography," 10 *Wayne Law Review* 655 (1964). They also argue that some of history's best-known sadists have been inspired not by obscenity but by otherwise respectable sources; for example, that the notorious British vampire John Haigh sucked his victims' blood through a straw and dissolved their drained bodies in acid after attending Anglican High Church services, or that Heinrich Pommerenke, Germany's mass rapist and woman-slayer, was prompted to his deeds by Cecil B. DeMille's *The Ten Commandments*. See Colin Wilson and Patricia Pitman, *The Encyclopedia of Murder* (New York: Putnam, 1961). To state the first argument is, in

different ways, a fact not to be forgotten in defining the dangers of obscenity or suggesting the cures. A recent study [12] revealed the phenomenon clearly enough:

		Sexual Response			
		Definite Frequent	Sometimes	Never	Number
		(%)	(%)	(%)	
Portrayals of nudes	Male	18	36	46	4191
	Female	3	9	88	5659
Observing genitalia	Male *	"Many"	"Many"	"Few"	
	Female	21	27	52	616
Commercial films	Male	6	30	64	3231
	Female	9	39	52	5698
Burlesques and floor shows	Male	28	34	38	3377
	Female	4	10	86	2550
Observing sex acts	Male	42	35	23	3868
	Female	14	18	68	2242
Engaging in coitus	Male	94	4	2	6115
	Female	79	10	11	5938
Reading literary materials	Male	21	38	41	3952
	Female	16	44	40	5699
Reading erotic stories	Male	16	31	53	4202
	Female	2	12	86	5523

* Percentages not reported.

America is, then, truly a melting pot of varying sexual responses. It is indeed difficult to envisage any society with such a divergence of responses which is not plagued by antisocial conduct resulting from at least some of these responses.

There are equally persuasive reasons for banning obscenity which need not rest on a foundation of statistics or the couch of a psychiatrist. Practical considerations do of

---

logical effect, to refute it; to make the second argument is to err by assuming that one or two examples justify defeat of a national policy as promising in its results as the outlawing of obscenity. Furthermore, if these men committed crimes of horror after contact with religious services or films of untrammeled virtue, the effects on the same men of exposure to obscene books would be explosive indeed.

12. 46 *Minnesota Law Review* 1009, 1020.

course exist; but we tend so often, in a world become pro-
gressively more pragmatic and computerized into moral
insensitivity, to close our eyes to original values. The most
cogent reason for banning obscenity may well be, quite
simply, its *a priori* moral wrongness. Pope Paul VI has perhaps most poignantly assailed the moral evil of eroticism:
"To be a man!—a level which should spare us the animal,
barbarous and subhuman degradations to which, still too
easily, yields our civilization no longer or not yet worthy of
the name." [13]

All our empirical studies, all our demographic data, all
our scientific methods threaten often to prevent America
from squeezing from the fruits of daily life the wine of a
new, assertive morality. It is ideologically facile, and
fashionable, to shy away from basic value judgments, and
turn instead to the transparent security of numbers, statistics, and diagrams. But the pioneers who sculpted the
basic American traditions and principles that defenders of
obscenity themselves espouse—inalienable rights, due process of law, freedom of expression—did not shirk the hard
questions; rather, they boldly etched the future of the
country with the indelible acid of ideals and principles. As
one panel of federal appellate judges has boldly held, "[T]he
great mass of the people still believe there is such a thing as
decency." [14]

The sense of morals which the Task Force endorses is
one which unembarrassedly supports the free and untrammeled moral growth of the nation's youth. We stand today
at a moral crossroads of sorts. The choice is, in a sense,
whether the development of America's young will be helped
or hampered by an exposure to obscenity as we know it today. The Task Force sees little to be gained by having
impressionable young minds set upon by what amounts,
really, to naked bodies in unseemly poses. There may perhaps be room for compromise. As the concept of obscenity

13. Quoted in *The New York Times*, October 2, 1969, p. 23.
14. *Besig v. United States*, 208 F.2d 142, 145 (9th Cir. 1953).
After all, "the American people are a clothed people." *Sunshine
Book Company v. Summerfield*, 128 F. Supp. 564, 569 (D.D.C. 1955).

as we know it today changes, as and if dirty pictures get cleaned and clothed, the effect on young people might not be so debilitating. We do not reject the chance for change, we welcome it. But until that change arrives, lines must be drawn; and it is from that responsibility that we cannot shirk.

The Task Force studied—as best we were able while at the same time respecting the reasonable bounds of privacy —the relationship between obscenity consumption and what used to be known, in a cleaner time, as real spiritual love. The inverse correlation is striking. The stark truth is that the greater the infusion of obscenity into a given community, the less real love in that community. Not surprisingly, the very physical characteristics of homes in communities with obscenity problems are sex-oriented. In many, bidets have been added to bathrooms; in others, double-sized baths; in others, red satin sheets hug provocatively sized and suggestively shaped beds. Can children ignore all this?

This catalog of moral considerations is not to suggest, of course, any lack of practical reasons for eliminating obscenity. It is axiomatic that obscenity breeds sexual excitation. The correlation between the rise of obscenity and the rise of both venereal disease and the threat of overpopulation is no less revealing than the crime correlation. The rise of obscenity has been documented earlier in this report. It is not mere coincidence that that rise parallels the national rise in venereal disease—highlighted by annual increases of 400 percent in Newark, New Orleans, Oakland, Long Beach, and Seattle, and of 100 percent in another seven eastern cities [15]—and the frightening national statistics reflecting population increases, presented in the tables on page 48.

The Task Force confidently reports that with no exceptions whatsoever,[16] greater frequency of sexual intercourse produces greater possibility of conception. If the incitement to intercourse provided by obscenity is effectively curtailed,

15. Hearings, p. 172.
16. Except one or two. See, for example, the so-called D'Orchamps exception, first reported in Lambert's monumental and still unpublished study of it.

United States Area and Population: 1790 to 1960 [17]

Area figures represent area on indicated date including in some cases considerable areas not then organized or settled, and not covered by the census. Area figures have been adjusted to bring them into agreement with remeasurements made in 1940.

Census date Conterminous U.S.*	Area (Square miles)	Number	Pop. Per Sq. Mile of Land Area	Increase over Preceding Census (No.)	(%)
1790 (Aug. 2)	888,811	3,929,214	4.5	(X)	(X)
1800 (Aug. 4)	888,811	5,308,483	6.1	1,379,269	35.1
1810 (Aug. 6)	1,716,003	7,239,881	4.3	1,931,398	36.4
1820 (Aug. 7)	1,788,006	9,638,453	5.5	2,398,572	33.1
1830 (June 1)	1,788,006	12,866,020	7.4	3,227,567	33.5
1840 (June 1)	1,788,006	17,069,453	9.8	4,203,433	32.7
1850 (June 1)	2,992,747	23,191,876	7.9	6,122,423	35.9
1860 (June 1)	3,022,387	31,443,321	10.6	8,251,445	35.6
1870 (June 1)	3,022,387	39,818,449	13.4	8,375,128	26.6
1880 (June 1)	3,022,387	50,155,783	16.9	10,337,334	26.0
1890 (June 1)	3,022,387	62,947,714	21.2	12,791,931	25.5
1900 (June 1)	3,022,387	75,994,575	25.6	13,046,861	20.7
1910 (Apr. 15)	3,022,387	91,972,266	31.0	15,997,691	21.0
1920 (Jan. 1)	3,022,387	105,710,620	35.6	13,738,354	14.9
1930 (Apr. 1)	3,022,387	122,775,046	41.2	17,064,426	16.1
1940 (Apr. 1)	3,022,387	131,669,275	44.2	8,894,229	7.2
1950 (Apr. 1)	3,022,387	150,697,361	50.7	19,028,086	14.5
1960 (Apr. 1)	3,022,387	178,464,236	60.1	27,766,875	18.4
1950 (Apr. 1)†	3,615,211	151,325,798	42.6	19,161,229	14.5
1960 (Apr. 1)‡	3,615,211	179,323,175	50.5	27,997,377	18.5

X Not applicable. * Excludes Alaska and Hawaii. † Revised to include adjustments for underenumeration in Southern States; unrevised number is 38,558,371. ‡ Includes Alaska and Hawaii.

Estimated Population of the United States [18]

Date	Inc. Armed Forces Overseas	Resident Population
1960 Census	180,007,000	179,323,175
July 1, 1961	183,756,000	183,057,000
July 1, 1962	186,656,000	185,890,000
July 1, 1963	189,417,000	188,658,000
July 1, 1964	192,120,000	191,372,000
July 1, 1965	194,592,000	193,815,000
July 1, 1966	196,907,000	195,923,000
July 1, 1967	199,114,000	197,859,000
July 1, 1968	201,152,000	199,846,000
July 1, 1969	203,216,000	201,921,000

17. *The 1970 World Almanac*, p. 253.
18. *Ibid.*, p. 310.

the population explosion can be curbed without extreme steps. Otherwise, the prospects are as gloomy as the problem is awesome. Already, conservation groups across the nation are suggesting that sexual activity be regulated by agencies patterned after existing federal boards. One concept gaining support and momentum in Rollipse, Iowa, is the distribution of intercourse coupons, nontransferable and redeemable for groceries. To the Commission, that idea is somewhat ahead of its time. But time may catch up.

Even more persuasive of the dangers of obscenity than broad truths carried by sociological statistics are case histories of individuals. The seventy-year-old matron who, after retiring to Arizona for reasons of health, received by mail an unsolicited advertisement so describing the joys of a new battery-run kit of prosthetic male genitalia that she raped a teen-age mailman; the federal funds so desperately needed to protect our wholesome overseas youths, diverted instead to help equip a little-known medical facility in the Black Hills of South Dakota named the Hospital for Excessive Onanism and Respiratory Ailments: these stories, and thousands like them all suggest forcefully the need to curb obscenity. We are aware, of course, that some well-meaning people have argued, in the words of Supreme Court Justice William O. Douglas, that "the First Amendment demands more than a horrible example or two of the perpetrator of a crime of sexual violence in whose pocket is found a pornographic book, before it allows the Nation to be saddled with a regime of censorship." [19] But such an argument misses the thrust of our position. In the first place, the Task Force does not advocate a "regime of censorship." To the contrary, we urge strict respect for and compliance with freedom of speech and expression. We merely ask for an end to obscenity.

More important than that misconception, however, is the cavalier disregard for the rights of individuals victimized by sex-crazed criminals who feed on obscenity. Consider whether the following actual situations were merely a "hor-

19. *Memoirs v. Massachusetts,* opinion of Mr. Justice Douglas, 383 U.S. 413, 432 (1966).

rible example or two" to the victims of these offenses and to their families: [20]

—the fifteen-year-old girl who became a prostitute after reading cheap novels glamorizing prostitutes' lives;
—the hitchhiker subjected to horrifying indecencies by men whose homes were virtual storehouses of obscenity;
—the thirteen-year-old girl who commits sodomy, or the boy scouts who encourage her to, or the young teen-age boys who engage in "round-robin" sodomy after reading obscene books;
—the sixteen-year-old with a proven case of syphilis;
—the tens of thousands of young boys and girls who open their mail only to find pictures of naked men and women.

Perhaps the spokesmen for obscenity regard those who sympathize with the plight of these people as "mealy-mouthed" or "wishy-washy." But how any sentient human being, how anyone aware of people's real goals and aspirations, real needs and pains, can simply turn aside and disregard these hard, cold facts as "simply an example or two" is difficult.

The picture of promiscuity in America is not a pretty one. Out-of-wedlock children comprised nearly 17 percent of all nonwhite births in America in 1940. By 1950 the figure mounted to 18 percent; by 1960, 21.6 percent; by 1966, 26.3 percent.[21] That such an unmistakable tendency is in large part attributable to lack of "those wise restraints" seems patently obvious. By curbing the spread of obscenity, we do not claim that the population explosion will be arrested; but that it can be significantly slowed seems clear. So, too, the

20. From Hearings, pp. 27, 41, 174; J. Edgar Hoover, "Combatting Merchants of Filth: The Role of the F.B.I.," 25 *University of Pittsburgh Law Review* 469 (1964).
21. *Civil Disorders Report*, p. 262. Interestingly, the generalization by the Crime Commission Report that "the offenses, the victims, and the offenders are found most frequently in the poorest and most deteriorated and socially disorganized areas of cities" (p. 35) does not apply in all cases to obscenity offenses. See p. 64.

promiscuity engendered by freely circulating obscenity cannot but have a substantial and deleterious effect upon propensity toward venereal disease. More selective mating, more concern for the health of one's sexual partner,[22] more respect for the sexual act itself, would follow the elimination of obscenity from our shores.

Indeed, in the words of Supreme Court Justice Clark, we are not "shrinking violets";[23] we share a deep respect for the importance of genuine sexual gratification. But obscenity is a sorry way of introducing the nation's youths to what is, in reality, one of life's beautiful experiences. Too often in our interviews with the youth of America, we were struck by an unmistakable callousness toward sexual commerce. Too often, sex was conceptualized and regarded as something dirty, something to be bought at a rundown newsstand, taken into a lavatory, and later discarded. That is simply wrong. We should be wary of leaving our children with a sexual heritage devoid of spiritual fulfillment and interpersonal gratification. Obscenity seems gradually and wrongfully to be replacing parents as the tutor for this important subject.

To portray the human form, modeled in God's own image, as a vessel of bestial gratification; to portray the acts of sex as cravings for sexual gratifications—surely our moral antennae are sensitive enough to condemn such perversions without having to search for measurable evidence of undesirable results. Can we not mourn the falling of a

22. To present a true picture of the real evils of obscenity, the Task Force has relied exclusively on plainly demonstrable data and proven examples. We do not advertise this catalog of harms as all-inclusive, however. Strong suggestions which have been made attributing other harms to the spread of obscenity merit strong attention, and may one day be scientifically established when resources permit intensive testing. Thus we note, without comment, the possibility of widespread "masturbatic insanity" should the flow of obscenity continue unabated. See G. Stanley Hall, 1 *Adolescence* 432 ff. (1921). Hall is not alone in his judgment. In the Hearings, Dr. Frignito noted that "most delinquents admit to more than average masturbation" (Hearings, p. 67).

23. Clark, J., dissenting in *Memoirs v. Massachusetts*, 383 U.S. 413, 441 (1966).

sparrow without first weighing the physical loss to mankind? Have we no moral soul? Indeed we believe we do. For the sake of our own moral integrity, if for no other reason, every American owes it to himself, to his family, to his religion, and to his local, state, and national governments, to do his part toward erasing the blot and blight which spread so quickly and heavily across the national morality.

Section 2: The Usages of Obscenity

HAVING, THEN, FOCUSED the inquiry by defining the nature of obscenity and concluding, indeed, that obscenity is an evil to be washed from the face of American life, the Task Force studied the actual usage of obscenity, personal, demographic, and economic. We were interested in discovering both why obscenity is patronized and the sociology of that patronage.

A HUMAN PORTRAIT

We live in a complex world, and we are a complex people. The reasons for the spread of obscenity are as complex as that world, and as we ourselves. There is no single reason for the cancerous spread of obscenity in America. The factors are as varied as our society is heterogeneous.

It would be easy, of course, having resolved to eliminate obscenity and having defined it to the point of recognition, simply to eliminate it from the American scene. But we are trampling on the desires, albeit illicit, of Americans with genuine rights; when and as we eliminate obscenity, therefore, we ought never to lose sight of the fact that we are dealing with real people, with real feelings, sensitivities, and urges. The Task Force therefore deemed it wise to isolate those factors which seem most frequently to drive people to obscenity, in the hope that an effective anti-obscenity campaign would, in recognizing the causes of obscenity offenses, be more effective in the fight while at the same time manifesting a real understanding for the erstwhile victims of obscenity, the obscenity consumer himself.

People resort to obscenity for many reasons.

The complexity of each American in today's diffuse, sophisticated society renders futile any attempts to quantify causal factors and meaningfully to weigh comparative causal pressures.[1] Nevertheless, certain causes reoccur regularly and with perfectly obvious relevance.

One of the most common reasons for Americans' resort to obscenity is the urge of sheer lust.[2] The Task Force has rather little to add to the comprehensive literature and psychology of lust, but the candid observations of various anthropologists and others should not be taken to detract from the significance of the lust factor in understanding the surge of obscenity. The lust motive seems to appear more frequently among the young than among the old. The reason may be merely physiological; then again, how many dirty magazines can you buy on a Social Security check? In the realm of obscenity, this country has demonstrated that peculiar American ability to translate a vision into reality, an ability more appropriate for self-congratulation in other spheres of potential accomplishment.

But lust, like life, cannot survive in a vacuum. Like any trait, it is a product of an environment, a climate, a soil. Were our less admirable strivations isolated characteristics,

1. The Task Force frankly admits its attempt and concedes its failure so to quantify. Field staffs in major cities throughout the country conducted extensive and intensive interviews in obscenity circles, gathering statistics on primary, secondary, and tertiary causes of resort to obscenity, and the relative importance ascribed to those causes by the users themselves. In addition, the Task Force itself provided psychiatric assistance to users willing to allow the Task Force access to those psychiatric reports. We were unable, however, either to process that data by computer or to synthesize the results into tables accurately reflecting the phenomena.

2. A near-truism the significance of which should not be obscured by its obviousness. As Desmond Morris has noted, "Clearly, the naked ape is the sexiest primate alive." *The Naked Ape* (New York: McGraw-Hill), 1968, p. 53.

they would die like flowers in sand. These baser urges, however, are nurtured by a permissive laxity the limits of which are difficult to perceive. This moral permissiveness is no less to blame than the lowly instincts which feed at its altar. We have spoken earlier of the "national malaise of lawlessness." [3] The societal permissiveness, the unwillingness to defend principle, the fear of "rocking the boat" all contribute to an atmosphere tolerant of an immorality as loose as Western civilization has ever produced.

Excessive permissiveness, then, in areas which at first blush may seem unrelated to the growing threat of obscenity, coalesces with basic lustful drives to produce one of the more glaring causes of people's resort to obscenity. For all our recognition of the contribution of general over-permissiveness, however, the Task Force does not minimize or underestimate the impact of lust itself as a spur to obscenity.[4]

Not unrelated to the general air of national permissiveness is a further cause of the American resort to obscenity. We have always been an adventuresome people. The pioneers who painstakingly worked their way from the large eastern ocean to the even larger western ocean left behind them, besides a tangible heritage marvelous to behold, a legacy of the spirit, a will to quest, to persevere, to discover, and to taste. Unfortunately, the enthusiasm of that legacy has reached beyond its optimal grasp. The singular American sense of excitement and curiosity, of seek and discover, has reached a point no longer wondrous to behold.

We do not mean to question the importance of these traits, either to our heritage or to our continuing success as a nation. We simply note, as an aid to understanding some of the reasons which underlie burgeoning obscenity rates, that the American impulse to pluck and taste of forbidden fruit, combined with a contemporary tendency and leniency toward general lawlessness, is a common cause of obscenity consumption.

3. See p. 42.
4. See Masters and Johnson, *Human Sexual Response* (Boston: Little, Brown, 1966).

It would be difficult to overemphasize the reality of the danger that, by overindulging our sexual and pornographic instincts, we may be subconsciously planting the seeds of our destruction as a society. Permissiveness has a way of expanding, as if it breathed a life of its own. In this regard it would not be unwise to apply Freudian psychoanalytic insights to our own future development as a nation: "Two kinds of instinct (outward aggressiveness and self-destruction) seldom—perhaps never—appear in isolation from each other, but are alloyed with each other in varying and very different proportions and so become unrecognizable to our judgment. . . . [M]asochism would be *a union between destructiveness directed inward and sexuality*—a union which makes what is otherwise an imperceptible trend into a conspicuous and tangible one." [5]

Reasons of lust do not by any means, however, wholly account for American consumption of obscenity. Painful social and economic pressures drive very many decent citizens, in all other respects law-abiding, into the lairs of obscenity purveyors. In slum and ghetto areas this is especially true. In those areas, housing is generally substandard. Many people live in poorly heated apartments; many buildings are so dilapidated and otherwise neglected as to provide breeding grounds for rats; many blocks provide little meaningful sanitation service. Can there be any wonder that those citizens turn for some small comfort to obscenity?

Significantly, so many of those same lower-income tenants are employed in jobs that provide little excitement, little chance for promotion, and little pay.[6] This is not to say that those inner-city residents are in any respect less equipped innately to handle more desirable jobs. They are the same people, however, who for the most part have been

5. Sigmund Freud, *Civilization and Its Discontents* (1930), Vol. 21, *The Standard Edition of the Complete Psychological Works of Sigmund Freud*, James Strachey, ed., *op. cit.*, p. 120.
6. Ths latter fact explains the Task Force's general experience that most obscenity sold in slum areas is less elaborate than that of most suburban communities.

educated at inferior schools and brought up in poorer homes by parents unable, through no fault of their own, to provide an ideal family background for later financial growth. They are also the same people who, with their families, eat low-quality food. They are the same people who live in the substandard housing described above. Can the victims of these circumstances really be blamed for resorting to obscenity as a placebo?

For these people, obscenity is very much like an opiate. It is not surprising that, in communities like these, obscenity should find a home among the same people as heroin. A respite, an escape: surely, those who turn to obscenity for these reasons are not perforce "bad" people, in the pejorative sense of "bad."

But our purpose here is not to blame, to criticize, or to condemn. Our purpose is simply to elucidate. Quite simply, people turn to obscenity for more than mere motives of lust. People turn to obscenity because they are products of their environment, and we as a nation have failed to produce a society whose standards of housing, employment, education, and nutrition are sufficient to sustain moral cleanliness. But let us make one thing perfectly clear: Having isolated the cause, we are optimistic about the cure.

The country does not lack, however, for persons eager to exploit the inclinations of the masses. The theory of our commercialism is such as to allow those who would "make a fast buck" by pandering to many Americans' weaknesses to do so with relative impunity. As the sociologist C. Wright Mills has commented, an "astounding volume of commodities . . . is addressed more often to the belly or to the groin than to the head or to the heart." [7] And the same tendency was noted by economist J. K. Galbraith.

The lack of capacity for self-restraint among certain sectors of an otherwise healthy economy is perhaps nowhere more pronounced than in the readiness of Madison Avenue advertisers to package obscenity in a manner appealing to

7. Mills, "On Knowledge and Power," in *Power, Politics, and People*, I. L. Horowitz ed. (New York: Oxford University Press, 1963), p. 671.

baser instincts. We need not cite examples here;[8] one need only scan the so-called entertainment section of any big-city newspaper to appreciate the essentially sexual nature of so much of today's entertainment as that entertainment is predescribed for the potential viewer. It is not surprising that one grows quickly jaded by the constant sight of revealing decolletage and revealed anatomy. Surely, there is more to commend much of America's cultural achievements than raw sexuality. Yet the greed of exploiters is such that one would, if otherwise unschooled, regard contemporary American culture as a breeding ground for sexual profligacy or, simply, a breeding ground.

One's constant exposure to this sort of thing, of course, quickly inures one, and incites one to even more provocative experience. "The medium is the massage," critic Marshall McLuhan has written, and America has indeed been massaged into moral nonchalance by its media. We do not question for a moment the continued vitality of private enterprise and its relevance to today's needs. We simply suggest that the exploiters both of human frailty and of the permissiveness of a highly developed capitalism should exercise a respectable quantum of self-restraint.

Nor should the advertising firms alone shoulder the blame for lack of self-discipline. The media themselves which provide a canvas for the advertising man's brush have shown a remarkable disdain for the responsibility freedom demands. The men behind the media are by no means typical Americans. They are "a small band of conspirators who choose news and commentary in a way designed to sell the liberal ideology of the New York-Washington axis." [9] It is not the role of our government to police the press, but it is not the role of the press to require policing. Not only has the press contributed to the upsurge of obscenity in America by hungrily inviting the shekels of pornography peddlers, though that in fact is a considerable sin; more importantly, the media in general have not given

8. See pp. 33 ff.
9. Vice-President Agnew, describing media, as paraphrased in *The New York Times Magazine*, January 11, 1970, p. 31.

fair coverage to the dangers of obscenity, thus creating among certain communities the unsound and unhealthy impression that obscenity is not only to be permitted but adored as a symbol of freedom of expression. As one Congresswoman, prominent in the fight against obscenity, has herself observed, "I think the press could do a better job editorial-wise." [10]

The media's disingenuousness in this regard stems no doubt from their sincerely held belief that no limitations on expression should be countenanced, and that once obscenity is curtailed, the ax of "censorship" may fall elsewhere. We share their concern for that eventuality, while at the same time assuring them that the concern is more theoretical than realistic. When we strive to eliminate obscenity, we strive not to strike at the heart of any reasonable form of expression. The obscenity toward which this Administration should unsheath its moral lance is not expression at all, but downright undeniable depictions of filth.

We trust that the specter of censorship is raised by the media in good faith through a mistaken belief in its dangers, rather than as a straw man with which to attack this Task Force's intentions. Nor do we suggest that the correction of the distorted picture of the relative vices and virtues of obscenity is properly the role of democratic government. We simply note the media's general tendency toward irresponsible coverage of obscenity in the expectation that, having been noted, the fault will be corrected.

One further cause for the popularity of obscenity deserves mention. Research in areas of sex, obscenity, and related matters is a widely spreading enterprise. Often, ambiguous tendencies result, none more schizophrenic than the unsuccessful attempt in 1956 by the federal government to prevent importation of pornographic materials by the Institute for Sex Research, Inc., toward whose projects the government itself had contributed over $150,000 in grants.[11]

There is nothing wrong with honest intellectual fulfill-

10. Rep. Katherine Granaham, quoted in Hearings, p. 187.
11. Pilpel and Zavin, *Rights and Writers*, (New York: Dutton 1960) pp. 327 ff.

ment, even where matters of obscenity are concerned. The Task Force wonders, however, whether those individuals and groups engaged in apparently scientific inquiries are being true to their own integrity, whether in fact much of what purports to be scientific study is really a respectable cover for the failure to adapt sexually in a normal manner. Many adult purchasers of obscenity whom the Task Force staff interviewed justified their actions as a modest form of intellectual curiosity.[12] Perhaps that explanation was best stated by a father of three who told us, "Our kids are growing up surrounded by 'obscenity,' and I feel I should know something about it. One can learn much of one's civilization from its literature."

We do not question the motives of such people, only the accuracy of their self-perception. That adult defense of resort to pornography is not unlike the child's plaint that marijuana is being sampled merely as an intellectual experience, "just to know what it's like." We should be wary of this type of self-deception, especially when it does provide such a convenient excuse for gratification of a powerful, if base, instinct.

There are, then, multiple reasons explaining Americans' resort to obscenity. All are understandable; most are condemnable; none are tolerable. All share the common factor of humanness. No matter our ideological persuasion, no matter the rightness of the cause: The cure, wherever it may be, must recognize the fact that as the cause lies in human nature, so must the cure.

12. The Task Force itself had access, of course, to vast quantities of obscenity while preparing this report. To prevent the Task Force's work from being self-defeating, we purchased and used second-hand original sources wherever possible to minimize the risk of providing a substantial original market for purveyors. These materials should be stored for five years in the National Archives, thereby allowing access to future critics of the report, and then destroyed.

A SOCIOLOGICAL PORTRAIT

Having isolated the personal reasons which turn Americans to obscenity, the Task Force sought to answer some basic sociological questions concerning the actual spread of the disease. The Task Force sought to learn whether obscenity is in fact on the rise; if so, where; and how obscenity is disseminated.

Obscenity is on the rise.

When President Nixon advised this Task Force that "Obscenity is a disease gnawing cancerously at the roots and hearts of America," [13] he was not joshing. Nor is the trend a new one, though the rise seems to be precipitously steep today. The Task Force has collated past studies, and has brought them up to date with its own studies, financed by federal funds allocated for our needs. Past statistical data, though sketchy when considered severally, present an unmistakable vision of rising obscenity when viewed in their entirety. The trend has been clear for some time. Examples abound.

In Philadelphia, prosecutions initiated by the Post Office Department increased from 106 to 127 for the time period July 1, 1961, to October 13, 1961, compared with the same time span the year before—a startling increase of 19.8 percent. Convictions also rose during that period, from 68 to 106, or an increase of 25.6 percent.[14] Although obscenity statistics *per se* are not available for earlier periods in that city, it is noteworthy that court cases of fornication, bastardy, and neglect rose 120.8 percent between 1949 and 1959, from 1,173 to 2,590.[15] For those to whom these latter

---

13. Others have, with comparable insight and eloquence, noted the same phenomenon. The late Justice Musmanno, for example, a jurist with a keen sense of national sociological currents, decried in 1965 the "wide river of filth . . . sweeping across the nation" (quoted in 65 *Yale Law Journal* 127, 157, fn. 138). The cancer has also been likened to a bog, a quagmire, a morass, and a pigsty.

14. Hearings, p. 127.

15. Hearings, p. 67.

data are unpersuasive regarding the rise of obscenity, a further datum of significance is the rise in the number of unwed mothers, between 1939 and 1962, from 300 to 5,000— a rise which the president judge of a Pennsylvania county court attributes, in 95 percent of the cases, to "willful and immoral acts" inspired by the aura of pornographic filth in the metropolitan area.[16] Perhaps even more significant, by 1962 nearly 2,000 Philadelphians were members of nudist organizations.[17]

The same trend is apparent in prosecutions initiated by the Post Office Department.[18] Arrests there for obscenity crimes rose from 201 in 1957 to 293 in 1958, climbing steadily, in succeeding years, to 315,389, and 457. Convictions climbed proportionately. In New York State alone, in fiscal 1961, no fewer than 4,724 obscenity complaints were filed, and 985 cases were actually instituted.

The national picture has been no more comforting. For the five years ending July 1, 1955, only 46 federal obscenity convictions were obtained. In the next five years, the number soared to 78 and punishment meted out for those 78 convictions totaled 230 years and $28,550. The FBI recently discovered that one indecent merchandiser had a list of over 400,000 names and addresses of prospective customers, many of them children. A raid of one pornographer's warehouse uncovered four tons of obscenity, including 8 million lewd pictures and cartoons.[19]

These figures, in microcosm, provided unmistakable handwriting on the wall for the survey the Task Force undertook to confirm the rise of obscenity in America.

We sought to determine the extent to which this increased consumption of obscenity reflected itself nationwide. To answer the inquiry, field staffers conducted detailed surveys in representative cities throughout the

16. Hearings, p. 63.
17. Hearings, p. 305.
18. Terence J. Murphy, *Censorship: Government and Obscenity* (New York: Taplinger), 1963, p. 191.
19. Hoover, 25 *University of Pittsburgh Law Review* 469, supra p. 50 fn. 20.

country. The results of their studies showed that, since 1900, obscenity in all major forms—literature, graphics, cinema, profanity—has spread in all areas of the nation.

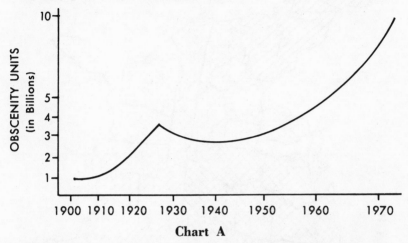

Chart A

Chart A reflects this overall rise. For quantitative analysis of the phenomenon, the Task Force equated one obscene book with one obscene movie or one obscene picture with one obscene phonograph record; such a scale, though not technically unchallengeable, seemed a fair method of quantification for comparative purposes, since each unit accomplishes its own result as an integrated whole, and since minor inaccuracies would tend to neutralize themselves over the long run. The data reflected in Chart A compellingly demonstrate that resort to obscenity has been increasing rapidly throughout the century, with the sole exception of the Depression years.[20]

The contemporary overall view of obscenity is remarkable if for no other reason than its revelation of the presence of obscenity throughout the country. Definite regional tendencies toward specialized obscenity media characterize the national picture as a whole. The Task Force's demographic studies of national obscenity trends uncovered the national predilections that are set forth in Chart B.

20. During which time money necessary to purchase obscenity was harder to come by.

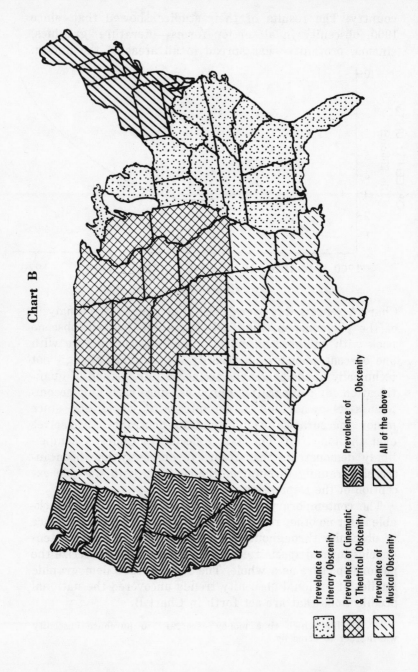

Chart B

Prevalence of
Literary Obscenity

Prevalence of
Cinematic
& Theatrical Obscenity

Prevalence of
Musical Obscenity

Prevalence of
—————— Obscenity

All of the above

Chart B reflects only those media in largest circulation in the denominated areas. It should not be interpreted to suggest that, for example, graphic obscenity is not a dangerous threat in the Northeast—only that literary obscenity is, when measured by obscenity units in circulation, the most rampant form of obscenity there. Indeed all media of obscenity may be found throughout the country, in sizable numbers. In fact, although literary obscenity is the most prevalent form of obscenity in the Northeast—not surprisingly, especially in view of the Northeastern control of most journalistic media—the per capita occurrence of dirty movies in the Northeast was slightly greater than the per capita occurrence of dirty movies in the Midwest, despite the essentially cinema-oriented nature of most Midwestern obscenity. The sorry truth is that obscenity in the Northeast, in virtually all forms, far outstrips that of any other section of the country.

California threatens, however, to give the Northeast a "run for the money." The number of obscenity units, in all forms, circulating in California has risen, in the last decade, from slightly under 40 million units to over 1 billion units—the steepest spiral for that time span among all the states. It may be noteworthy that the precipitous rise strongly parallels the rise of certain extremist groups of nihilists in America. As one uncompromisingly liberal study has confessed, "The [Students for a Democratic] Society dates its establishment from a convention held in June 1962, at Port Huron, Michigan. The initial membership was about 200 activists. Since 1962, the membership has jumped to perhaps 20,000, grouped in several hundred campus chapters." [21]

As noted earlier, crimes of obscenity are evenhanded in their evil, afflicting ghetto and slum areas no more than middle- and upper-class suburbs.[22] There is simply no demonstrable correlation between population density and per capita obscenity consumption. It was not always thus. Task

21. *Report of the Fact-Finding Commission Appointed to Investigate the Disturbances at Columbia University in April and May 1968 (The Cox Commission Report)*, 1968, p. 55.
22. Compare Crime Commission Report, Chapter 2.

Force historians computed the relationship between obscenity consumption of representative cities of differing population sizes in 1944, and compared them with statistics compiled for those cities in 1969.

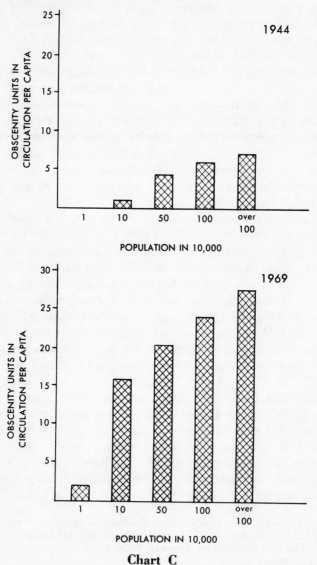

Chart C

It would be wrong, then, to regard obscenity as merely a plague of those forced to live in congested areas, accurate as such a judgment may have been some twenty-five years ago. Nor does any one form of obscenity predominate in any measurable degree in urban, metropolitan, or rural areas, although slum residents do frequently receive an inferior overall product (for example, binding on pornographic literature sold to ghetto patrons is noticeably cheaper than that sold to their suburban counterparts). But as one seller whom the Task Force interviewed noted: "Smut's as hot in a manila envelope as in a gold frame."

Viewed particularly, the situation is no less staggering than viewed broadly. Baths of potential corruption litter the beauty of American enterprise, and soil its traditions. Of the multitude of obscenity shops across the nation, many shine as veritable filth spas. To assist enforcement efforts and best allow concentration of cleansing resources where the need is greatest, the Task Force has isolated several shops as the dirtiest retailers in the country:

"Andre's Place" ****; formerly "Andre's"; 9th Street and McDermott Avenue, Los Angeles, California; run by Andre, the so-called "Faerie Queene"; pipes in soothing Muzak throughout a converted townhouse used to house seemingly endless shelves of pornographic books, both hard-core and paperback; gives plaid stamps for purchases over $2.95.

"The Imagination" ****; Elberton and Basin Streets, New Orleans, Louisiana; one of the world's most sophisticated pornography parlors; for those browsing through its famous basement art gallery, serves excellent coffee for 15¢, bottomless cup; *Cue* Magazine says, "For sheer luxury in exciting browsing, leave it to 'The Imagination.'"

"Four-Play" ***; Broadway and 43rd Street, New York City; so named for rich variety of magazines, stag films, statuary, and interpretive sketches; besides providing gourmet's delight to select from, cashier touches hand in giving change.

"The Coast Is Clear" **; ten miles outside Philadelphia along Pennsylvania Turnpike, concession inside Howard Johnson building; a rich selection of suggestive souvenirs from the City of Brotherly Love; provides spotless bathrooms with freshly sanitized toilet seats, all inspected weekly by the AAA; features crayons for temporary graffiti on stall doors.

"Harsh Realities" **; Elm and Main Streets, Denver, Colorado; one of the few American shops specializing in dirty picture postcards; imported the devilish postcard series "Deeds of Trust"; first smut shop to operate computer dating service.

****Highly recommended.
***Recommended.
**Interesting.

Although these are the worst offenders, they are supported by a cast of thousands, nationwide.

Just as it would be inaccurate to consider obscenity a limited geographic occurrence, so too would it be wrong to regard obscenity as simply a seasonal phenomenon.[23] Although more prevalent in some forms at some times than at others, obscenity exists in much the same way as the weather: It's always there, but sometimes there's more of it. Many people have asked: Just when does obscenity occur? To resolve that widely asked question, the Task Force undertook a comprehensive study of the frequency of occurrence of obscenity in various media at various times, with the results as shown in Chart D.

It is, thus, fair to say that although obscenity of a given type will at a given time sometimes glut the obscenity market, other types will glut the market at other times.

23. A mistake popularized in, e.g., *The Falling Leaves: A Seasonal Solution to Problems of Pornography* by Ormand Dunbarton (1968); *Flesh Famine: A Modest Proposal* by "Big Ralph" Mockridge (1967).

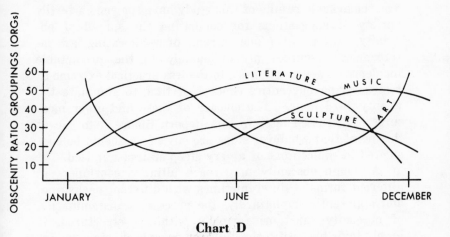

Chart D

Variations among media were absent, however, in the hourly breakdown. The dirtiest hour in the nation, obscenity-wise, is between ten and eleven P.M. As one distributor in downtown Chicago told the Task Force, "Give me just the ten-o'clockers and I'd cover expenses. The rest is gravy." Indeed, obscenity consumption builds from an extremely low early-morning level, swells slowly through the afternoon, and climaxes suddenly during the ten P.M. hour, subsiding peacefully afterwards, as shown in Chart E.

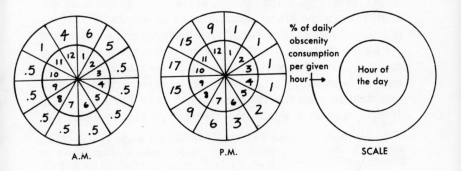

Chart E

The remarkable results of this study have spawned a fertile variety of suggestions for combating the spread of obscenity, ranging from one extreme of re-allocating law enforcement resources proportionately to the predictable incidence of hourly offenses, to the less practical extreme of restructuring our entire concept of time to eliminate the twenty-third hour.[24] The efficacy of these and other measures is discussed later in this Report. Suffice it to say at this point that whatever steps are envisaged should be considered in the context of a very steep staircase indeed.

Although obscenity may reach ultimate consumers in different forms at different times with different packaging, and apparently haphazardly, the process of dissemination of obscenity functions formally within a structured, if highly invisible, institution. Just as organized crime has infiltrated other legitimate and illegitimate businesses which promise large financial rewards, so it has seized control of the distribution of obscenity. The Department of Justice allowed the Task Force access to its heretofore classified information concerning distribution of obscenity and control of its markets. The files are revealing.

Domestic production and distribution of obscenity is, of course, big business. Government agents who have penetrated the veil of secrecy surrounding production have, with the aid of informants, estimated the number of obscenity units produced annually at nearly thirteen billion.

By subtracting the known domestic production of obscenity from the known total amount of obscenity in circulation in America, federal officials have estimated that over 3.8 billion units of obscenity are smuggled into the country annually. On the average, less than one-twentieth of this amount is seized by all enforcement agencies combined. The principal foreign sources are thought to be Paris and Scandinavia, and to a much lesser extent Mexico and the Far

24. A similar concept was suggested several years ago by Wintvrieden in his underground essay "New Organic Approaches to Obscenity." His thesis—that the high incidence of Friday-night obscenity dissemination justifies eliminating Fridays from the calendar —was substantially undermined by the Task Force's finding that, in fact, Tuesday is the dirtiest day (but not by much).

East. In most of those countries, obscenity is sold legally; but a substantial amount is diverted from local consumption to the black market, where it brings at least double the price. In Mexico, the production of obscenity is itself illicit, and takes place in remote mountainous terrain.

The finished product is smuggled into the United States either directly or indirectly through Canada, and proceeds on its way to the consumer. It becomes more expensive, of course, as it moves through the illicit channels of distribution. The same twelve-pack of French postcards depicting fellatio and cunnilingus which sells for twenty francs ($4) at a Paris newsstand may cost a suburban businessman in America as much as $100 after deviously wending its way around legal strictures.

A business of such significant volume and complexity requires sophisticated executives, for which organized criminal syndicates do not lack. At one time, obscenity was marketed competitively under the invisible but sure hand of private enterprise. Then, just as the Mafia has succeeded in other areas, unsuspecting private entrepreneurs suddenly found themselves with silent partners who shared the profits, basked beneath a roof of legitimacy, and rendered little service beyond supply. One typical proprietor of a "ma-and-pa" type obscenity concession described for the Task Force, in closed session and under a promise of anonymity, the method used by the Mafia to infiltrate an obscenity shop which, because of its unsophisticated organization, had been operating barely in the black.

John Doe, white, male, age seventy-two, had for nearly three decades been selling obscene literature of all sorts. He had established a reliable clientele through various innovations compatible with the temper of the times. A supplier, whom Doe refused to identify (for reasons the Task Force understood and respected), confided to Doe that shipments of color photographs depicting various acts of sadism and masochism never before seen in America had recently docked in New York harbor, the arena for much underworld activity. Eager to capture and control a promising market, but unable to provide the cash and unwilling to apply for an ordinary bank loan, Doe arranged through his illicit supplier a "six-for-five" loan. But after several months of lean sales, Doe was unable to satisfy payments regularly. As a consequence, the supplier became an unwanted half-partner in Doe's business. Once entrenched in the local obscenity trade at a retail level, the Mafia, by strong-arm and anti-competitive devices, was able to gain an exclusive neighborhood market and, thus, fixed prices at exorbitant levels.

As sophisticated as the processes of dissemination of obscenity may be, however, the final link in the distributional chain is the consumer—the American engaged in unlawful activity. Every consumer's illicit desires are nurtured, of course, by the salaciousness which generally pervades contemporary American culture, a salaciousness subtly encouraged by advertisements and materialism no less reprehensible than the underlying permissiveness to which we as a culture are succumbing. But in the final analysis, people are the real reason for the spread of obscenity; and it is people who must be cured. As the President has himself observed:

> The ultimate answer lies not with the government but with the people. What is required is a citizens' crusade against the obscene. When indecent books no longer find a market, when pornographic films can no longer draw an audience, when obscene plays open to empty houses, then the tide will turn. Government can maintain the dikes against obscenity, but only people can turn the tide.[25]

25. From President Nixon's Message to the Congress Proposing Legislation to Protect the Citizen from Receipt of Offensive Materials, May 2, 1969.

PART III

THE CONTROL OF OBSCENITY

Section 1: Historical Attempts

NO EVIDENCE OF the pornographic can be found at the Creation. For some four billion years thereafter, pornography was not observed on earth. Hence it is concluded that pornography is of relatively recent origin. In fact, the first recorded instance of obscene behavior seems to be that of Rhonda Ga'Resh, a Babylonian peasant maiden who was said to have bared her buttocks to the first sectional, second regional seer and revenue collector in order to avoid the spring payments. Their subsequent death by disemboweling may seem not entirely proportionate to the crime, but most historians, considering that the point of innovation is the most dangerous crime, concur in the general belief as to the gravity of the act, if not in the method of controlling it.

Beyond this, origins of obscenity are obscure and are shrouded in the mist of mankind's beginnings. Of course, as long as the overwhelming part of the populace was illiterate, obscene literature presented little real problem among the lower classes generally.

Among the upper classes it should not be supposed that the practice of pornography was an isolated adventure of the more barbarian nations of the world. To be sure, the Chinese were particularly adept at writing highly refined pornography, but the African tribesman—owing to his incapacity for true monarchy—virtually rejected any signs of pornographic addiction. The Europeans, on the other hand, developed pornography to its finest state, chiefly because even after the nonroyal acquired an education, pornography remained in the hands of the crown as a royal monopoly. The great pornographic art of medieval Europe did not come from the brushes of rank amateurs.

It was in England that pornography grew to its highest —or lowest—state, French and Flemish claims to the contrary notwithstanding. Owing partly to the Scandinavian influence and partly to the Germanic belief that life is better served by fantasy than life, the English earlier accustomed their kings and queens to the most comprehensive pornographic work. They outdid even the later Roman empresses, some of whom were said to have attended outdoor sporting events entirely naked and, spreading breadcrumbs on their abdomens, invited birds in the reviewing stands to feed from their navels.[1] Though the modern mind might find cause to be repelled by such an act, it should be remembered that the binocular had not yet been invented and therefore privacy was reasonably secure as to everyone but those immediately surrounding the royal box.

The great Renaissance paintings, some of which were deliberately pornographic, were not put out on public display, but hung in the reserved quiet of the great homes of the nobles. In view of the fact that the first reported case of obscene *conduct* to come before the British courts was not until 1663,[2] it is not surprising that attempts at control of obscene literature took much longer to develop. Sir Charles Sedley was an intimate of King Charles II, and his drinking activities reached their height in June 1663. As a contemporary then described it:

In the month of June 1663 this our author, Sir Ch. Sedley, Charles Lord Buckhurst (afterwards Earl of Middlesex), Sir Tho. Ogle, etc., were at a cook's house at the sign of the Cock in Bow Street near Covent Garden, within the liberty of Westm. and being inflam'ed with strong liquors, they went into the balcony belonging to that house, and putting

1. See, for example, Procopius' *Secret History* in connection with Empress Theodora's sporting proclivities.
2. *The King v. Sir Charles Sedley*, reported differently as *Le Roy v. Sr. Charles Sidney*, 1 Sid. 168 (K. B. 1663), and *Sir Charles Sydlyes Case*, 1 Keble 620 (K. B. 1663).

down their breeches they excrementiz'd in the street: which being done, Sedley stripped himself naked, and with eloquence preached blasphemy to the people; whereupon a riot being raised, the people became very clamorous, and would have forced the door next to the street open: but being hindered, the preacher and his company were pelted into their room, and the windows belonging thereunto were broken. This frolick thing being soon spread abroad, especially by the fanatical party who aggravated it to the utmost, by making it the most scandalous thing in nature, and nothing more reproachful to religion than that, the said company were summoned to the court of justice in Westminster Hall, where being indicted of a riot before Sir Rob. Hyde, lord chief justice of the common pleas, were all fined, and Sir Charles being fined £500, he made answer that he thought he was the first man that paid for shitting.[3]

Judicial mechanisms were created initially to curb the seditious and the blasphemous; injunctions could be issued to stop the publication or distribution of either; criminal penalties could be imposed on the writer or seller. But the law against the publication of obscenity was a comparatively late development. Censorship of books had been lodged by the Tudors in the infamous Court of Star Chamber, ultimately abolished in 1640 by the Long Parliament. Three years later a licensing law was enacted and continued, following Charles II's ascension to the throne, in the Licensing Act of 1662, which prohibited "heretical, seditious, schismatical, or offensive books or pamphlets." But this Act was aimed chiefly at obscene works, of which there were a number in wide circulation, and not only books but music—the madrigal was a famous example which has come to us greatly expurgated today.

Prior to the 1670's, then, owing chiefly to the influence of certain writers from a time gone by, the English language contained a great wealth of words that generally

3. Anthony A. Wood, *Athenae Oxoniensus*, IV, p. 731 (1813–1820). Quoted in Alec Craig, *Suppressed Books* (New York: Meridian, 1966), pp. 23–24. Much of the following discussion is based on Craig and like acounts.

offended even such liberal ears as King Charles's. These
words were not merely in the plays of great dramatists
where the low becomes art; they were, more significantly,
on the lips of rude folks everywhere. To His Majesty's min-
isters, decline and fall must inevitably follow the use by
young ladies of such words as "scral," "mepho," and the
still unprintable "s----f." Daily from 1665 these words and
others could be heard plainly on the streets from Parliament
to the palace. In March 1671, a young woman known only
as "the Canary" was arrested on the Strand for accosting
a silk merchant in words to this effect: "An' Bilfey, would
you see my scral and a quid for s----f?" Sentenced to thirty
years and a day by a tenderhearted judge (who could have
condemned her to intestinal puncture but was reputed to
have known her personally), the Canary begged for parole
on the grounds that this was her first offense and those
were the only words she knew for the carrying on of her
particular trade. In a moving letter to the King (the document was lost in 1688) the Canary evidently persuaded the
master of royal mercy for release. She became a court at-
tendant and for one year and more seemed genuinely
rehabilitated.

It is not to be supposed, then, merely because the Canary
was heard by the Archbishop of Canterbury to use the most
scrofulous language as he passed by the royal bedchamber
on the evening of April 6, 1672, that the Great Word Purge
did not have other, deeper causes. The Canary provided the
spark, to be sure, but the flame persisted long after; for as
many historians have pointed out, the people had provided
the dry kindling wood of obscenity. In view of the overwhelming pornographic content of English then used, it is
not surprising that the fury was directed at the indiscrimi-
nate use of the profane. No less than 367 obscene words
were first placed upon His Majesty's list and then ruthlessly
obliterated from the consciousness of the kingdom by the
simple expedient of putting to death those who used them.
Since the rule was uniformly applied, witch trials like those
shortly to begin in one of the colonies were avoided: The

accuser who uttered the proof, no less than the guilty who committed the crime, was sent to the gallows.

It is worthy of note, in view of the apprehension some people express today about internal security legislation and the like, that the Word Purge was strictly confined by the Attorney General and the Lord Keeper of the List to words and not to acts. To be sure, in its earliest days, many unattached women and even some wives were convicted on the theory that certain motions performed in the dark of night were symbolic (though silent) representations of the words condemned by law. But a courageous opinion in Hilary Term by Baron Rupert de Goff-Smith of the King's Bench clearly distinguished between words and deed and the King was much relieved.[4]

In 1695 the Licensing Act expired. There was then no legal authority to ban obscene books, as Mr. Justice Powell sadly lamented thirteen years later in a case in which he concluded that the printer of *The Fifteen Plagues of a Maidenhead* could not be subjected to criminal prosecution.[5] It was to be nineteen years before the King's Bench would proclaim it a common-law offense to publish an "obscene libel." [6] Even so, the law was rarely applied. Such a book as *Memoirs of a Woman of Pleasure (Fanny Hill)* circulated freely upon its publication in 1749.

Yet it was in this same century that the dramatic change in English social life transformed thought in relation to matters sexual, with a corresponding impact on the colonies that were shortly to declare political independence. Before the century was out, the law had taken a dim view of licentious publications. Certainly the proclamation against vice by King George III in 1787 helped turn the tide. By 1802 the English Society for the Suppression of Vice (not to be confused with the later American society of the same name) was formed and warred vigorously against the obscene. In-

4. *In the Matter of Ellen a Strumpet*, 4 Clq. 609 (K. B. 1672).
5. *Reg. v. Read*, 11 Mod. Rep. 142 (Q. B. 1707).
6. In the case of *Rex v. Curll*, 2 Stra. 788 (1727), for publication of *Venus in the Cloister or the Nun in Her Smock*.

terestingly, however, the chief means of control during the early nineteenth century was the actual *rewriting* of many classic works and others when they touched on dangerous ground. Most famous for this means of control was Dr. Thomas Bowdler,[7] whose very name has come to mean the expurgating and rewriting—bowdlerizing—of some of the most famous works of literature, Shakespeare and the Bible not excepted. It is generally conceded that Dr. Bowdler went too far. The spirit of bowdlerism caused changes from the original that would cause no one to cringe today.

In 1868 Lord Chief Justice Cockburn laid down a test of obscenity which endured for a long while and influenced American courts as well: "Whether the tendency of the matter charged as obscenity is to deprave and corrupt those whose minds are open to such immoral influences and into whose hands a publication of this sort may fall."

The separate strands of royal "Establishment" pornographic literature and the natural unfettered obscenity of the peasant bourgeoisie began to merge during the rise of mass literacy in the nineteenth century. As the inexorable pressure for universal literacy pressed on the Western educational system, names were necessarily given to some acts which peasants had been wordlessly performing for centuries. Many Western economists have rationalized the need for literacy by supposing that the relentless demand for industrialization required at least the functional ability to follow directions on the can. Indeed, we suppose no particular reason to dispute the grand capitalist tradition of which we are an integral part, but it is prudent to note that it is one of the ironies modern life is capable of mustering that

7. A recent authority has suggested that it was actually Dr. Bowdler's sister who was responsible for much of the rewriting, but that her name (Harriett) was not used because people would naturally be curious why if it did not affect her to read the original it would affect anyone else. See Noel Perrin, *Dr. Bowdler's Legacy* (New York: Atheneum, 1969). It is heartening to note that this kind of false shame is unnecessary today: The Maryland Board of Censors, for instance, is made up of housewives, and no one suggests that these women are perverted by what they must see in their previewing of all movies shown in the state.

capitalism is a major reason for the spread of pornography.[8]

The definite proof that pornography and peasant obscenity had teamed up came with archaeological discoveries of the past decade. From the revelation that underground smut books proliferated in later Victorian times, it has become abundantly clear that the Establishment hold on the hard-core dirty book had been broken. Spilling out to the British countryside, the waves of pornography and obscenity splashed together to wet the sands of the first "smut revolution." Not quite yet did the sand surface; it lay matted from Dunkirk to Ulster, but it remained only for the enterprising to recognize that there was an enormous market in the lusty prodigy of pornography and obscenity. It remained, in short, for the entrepreneurial genius of Americans to set the world on fire.

The American character is not natively conducive to smut.[9] In fact, the native American character may be conducive to nothing—a blank slate written on by the irresistible lure of the frontier that beckoned its pioneers. So much is legend with which it would do us scarce good to tamper at this late date. At any rate, it is tolerably clear that pornography and obscenity were not native impulses.

Records do support the proposition that smut was an early émigré to North American shores. Indeed, papers on deposit in the federal archives in Washington indicate that the captain of the Mayflower swore long and profanely during a storm off the Massachusetts cape. And certainly the long trains of slaves were no strangers to unnatural peasant acts, though they were probably unfamiliar with pornography.

At any rate, by the end of the Civil War, peasant acts had spread to all sections of the country. By 1884 they had

8. As to whether pornography is one of the anomalous cases, like lighthouses and antitrust, which require governmental intervention in the market, we express no opinion, it not being required of us at present.

9. Excepting the Indians, of course. The characteristic fertility dances of the Plains Indians caused kidnapped white women, we are informed, who first witnessed the dances between 1627 and 1882, to swoon.

so far taken hold of the popular imagination that Grover
Cleveland was able to capture the White House despite the
acknowledgment that he had fathered an illegitimate child,
and no one has ever known what else. Cleveland was a
Democrat.

The cowboy took it west. It is not to be supposed that
the popular image of the cowboy on the television screen
conforms to historical fact. Doubtless some cowhands slept
with their horses! But most of them were impatient for
pleasures they had learned in Texas. These in turn were
transmitted to certain women on the west coast who, when
the cows were being herded to the stockyards, consorted
with retail merchants and others, further transmitting the
peasant acts, heretofore noted.

The release of energy following World War I further
aggravated the erotic impulse. Flappers were ballyhooed.
Smut became American. That films, art, and books in the
1960's were to depict what the flapper hardly dared to
imagine is anticlimactic and quite beside the point. As the
images of nude men and women spread before the blinking
eyes of a hushed America—threatening to bed down to stay
—the nation scarcely recalled Rhonda Ga'Resh.

With this history in mind, it is not surprising to learn
that the path of censorship in America paralleled that in
England rather closely. States enacted legislation early in
the nineteenth century against obscene libel; federal legislation against imported smut was enacted in 1842 and
against sending smut through the mail in 1865.

The principal weapon against the published and pictured
obscenity from 1870 to 1930 was not the abstract law, however; it was the vigorous and personal intervention in the
law of Anthony Comstock and his successor, John S.
Sumner, both being secretary of the New York Society for
the Suppression of Vice. These men single-mindedly and
wholeheartedly waged an intensive campaign against literary and pictorial obscenity.

In the beginning it was entirely successful. Comstock's
slogan was "Morals, not Art or Literature." He was responsible for the Comstock Act, in 1873, bringing contraceptive

literature within the sexual prohibitions of the law. Scores of books fell prey to his relentless campaign; America was purified.

Unfortunately, as is often the case with dedicated people, Comstock and Sumner went a little to extremes. Any person who leads a life pledged to end a particular evil—especially if it is a moral evil—is always subject to the danger that his passion will carry him to excess, especially if he lacks any saving humor. Given the evil against which Comstock and Sumner chose to do battle, it was impossible to retain humor, and as a result they grew a little overzealous. Although still in 1929 Sumner was able to have banned in Massachusetts such books as Bertrand Russell's *What I Believe*, Sinclair Lewis' *Elmer Gantry*, and Ernest Hemingway's *The Sun Also Rises*, his power was fast waning.

Comstock had risen to the height of his power in 1915, the year he died, when President Wilson appointed him the United States delegate to the International Purity Congress in San Francisco. In that same year, Margaret Sanger's husband was indicted for giving some of his wife's articles on birth control to an agent sent by Comstock, who testified at the trial and died shortly thereafter. It was a portent.

Margaret Sanger was indicted and acquitted in 1916. In 1917, Sumner tried to stop sales of the translation of Gautier's *Mademoiselle de Maupin*, only to find the tables turned and the New York Court of Appeals affirming a conviction against him for malicious prosecution. He could not censor Flaubert or Gide or even Erskine Caldwell.[10] Though the case against the seller of Dreiser's *An American Tragedy* was upheld in Massachusetts. the case against Cabell's *Jurgen* was dismissed in New York.

Then in 1933, the mortal blow was struck against Comstock and Sumner, though their shades did not give up the ghost for more than a generation. In 1933 James Joyce's famed (then infamous) *Ulysses* went on trial after its importation into the United States. In a widely heralded opinion, District Judge Woolsey of the Federal Court in

10. *New York v. Viking Press, Inc.*, 147 Misc. 813, 264 N. Y. Supp. 534 (Sup. Ct. 1933).

New York reviewed the book and found it not obscene, though it contains some of the most disgusting words known to the English language. In essence, Judge Woolsey rejected Lord Chief Justice Cockburn's ruling that what a book contains is not the test: What is at issue, as clarified by the Court of Appeals which affirmed Judge Woolsey, is the dominant effect of the book as a whole. If it does not tend to promote lust, it is not legally obscene. Furthermore, the law is concerned with the normal or average person, not the abnormal one for whom a naked piano leg is sufficient cause to blush.[11]

The march of the courts was steady, though John Sumner courageously fought the immoral as late as 1948, when he succeeded in having Edmund Wilson's *The Memoirs of Hecate County* banned in New York.[12]

In 1957 the Supreme Court announced in *Roth v. United States* [13] that obscenity was not constitutionally protected by the First Amendment, a judgment, it is worth noting, the Court has never seen fit to reverse. The Court went on to say, however, that "sex and obscenity are not synonymous. Obscene material is material which deals with sex in a manner appealing to prurient interest." The Court also noted that it must appeal to the prurient interest of the average person, not the most susceptible. The bookseller's conviction in *Roth* was affirmed.

Nonetheless, booksellers became bolder. Always under the guise that their books contained socially redeeming ideas, they spewed forth with such as *Tropic of Cancer* and *Lady Chatterley's Lover*.

In 1966 the current standards were evolved. As we have noted earlier,[14] the Court has concocted a threefold test: (1) dominant-theme test; (2) patently-offensive test; and (3) utterly-without-redeeming-social-value test. And though, as we have noted, these tests are identical to standard

11. *United States v. One Book Entitled Ulysses*, 5 F. Supp. 182 (S.D.N.Y. 1933), *aff'd* 72 F.2d 705 (2d Cir. 1934).
12. The Supreme Court upheld the ban by an equally divided court in *Doubleday and Co. v. New York*, 335 U.S. 48 (1948).
13. *Roth v. United States*, 354 U.S. 476 (1957).
14. See p. 17.

nonlegal definitions, the courts have misapplied them. Thus, for instance, *Fanny Hill* has been permitted, and in a very recent case the Supreme Court has even allowed anybody to possess *any* book in the privacy of his or her home.[15]

It is interesting to note that the progression of methods of control has come full circle. Originally there was no control. Then the courts struck at lascivious and disgusting thoughts and language, and then they banned outright books which suggested certain kinds of immorality. Then the tide went out again, and first ideas were permitted to circulate, then books with lascivious and disgusting language were permitted for sale, and finally, as the courts have usually applied the tests today, there is no more control. The circle is complete.

15. The *Ginzburg* case, 383 U.S. 463 (1966), should be noted as an exception to the trend, for it held that in a close case, evidence that an author or publisher pandered to prurient interest in advertisements could prove the work obscene. *Stanley v. Georgia*, 394 U.S. 557 (1969).

Section 2: The Limits of Censorship

FROM THE FOREGOING, it is clear that the courts have been seeking a way to reconcile our nation's traditional interest in the freedom of citizens to speak out in public and in print with its equal interest in preserving the purity of that which is spoken or printed. It is a difficult task, and we do not offer criticism of the courts under the impression that it is easy. While we do assert the power of the people to censor out the obscene and pornographic, we realize that there must be limits to the censor's power, else we lose much that is wholesome as well as that which is not. But there must be some control. We believe that if obscenity is properly defined and the purpose for censorship fixed in mind, a practical solution is possible.

First, we wish to prevent the circulation of only that which is obscene, *because* we wish to curb violent crimes that come in its wake. Given that as the national goal, a legal policy toward pornographic censorship can be fashioned. Second, it follows, therefore, that we wish to censor only that which *causes* the tendency toward violence and crime. Obviously, if there are works which by some standards are "pornographic" but which in fact would never incite anyone to commit antisocial acts, there can be no real harm. That should be patent.

IDEAS VERSUS ENTERTAINMENT

One way to reach discernible limits of censorship is to note that the purpose of the First Amendment is to protect the advancing of ideas. Insofar as a book or article is just a story and no ideas are advocated, there can never be a problem; otherwise, ritual murder could be equally justified as "entertainment." The concept of entertainment does not appear to have any absolute constitutional protection. Thus, to take a concrete example, James Joyce's *Ulysses,* though it has some passages within it which might by themselves qualify as obscene, cannot be as a whole obscene because it is not an entertaining book. Consequently it has not been declared unfit to read.

Now, this is a concept capable of some abuse. Recall that we defined obscenity as that which falls under two principal heads: that which titillates and that which disgusts. Someone will be quick to point out, no doubt, that that which disgusts is not entertaining either, and therefore it must receive constitutional protection. We would not go that far. For what disgusts some doubtless arouses others. There is, in fact, no surer proof than that there *are* disgusting books, pictures, and movies purveyed today. Thus the mere fact that disgust is aroused in some is not enough to classify the matter as non-entertainment. This distinction, incidentally, also answers the dilemma that is sometimes posed by those who argue that if the particular matter is disgusting then it cannot incite anyone to action, and if it cannot produce the requisite incitement the constitutional basis on which it is prohibited falls. The answer clearly is as stated above: That which disgusts some will always arouse others to the level of an incitement.

It is on this "development of incitement" that the limits of censorship can be discerned. For it has long been a fundamental of our criminal law that that which incites others to crime can itself be a criminal act. Those who advocate the overthrow of the government by force and violence and other unlawful means can be criminally punished for inciting others to such action. Likewise, those who incite riots by fiery and impassioned speeches and preaching can be jailed. There need be no qualms then about prohibitions against the publication and circulation of obscenity, since it is clear that such matter incites many people to crime. In all of the fifty States, as well as the District of Columbia, local laws extensively and expansively make a host of sexual perversions criminal acts. There can be no doubt that it would be the height of folly to ban the acts, on the one hand, but not the very writings and pictures which lead people on to performing them. And certainly the public should have protection from assault and rape.

Of course, we should not go too far. One might lawfully advocate changing the national leadership through peaceful means and find that a crazed follower resorts to violence to achieve this otherwise lawful (and sometimes laudable) goal. The mere fact, in other words, that the causal chain ultimately goes back to the published work, is not in itself reason to censor. We need a theory to limit banning, for we must be ever mindful of the inexorables.

This theory, in the realm of obscenity, is at hand. *For there can be no legitimate purpose in a work that incites to crime if the work itself is obscene.* Two elements must coalesce: the work must itself be obscene, and it must cause the necessary incitement. Thus, to take an example on the one extreme: If an insane person, having read the Bible, were to commit a crime and blame it on his reading of the Scriptures, we could not for that reason ban the Biblical texts. For although the causal chain may have been present, the book itself is not obscene. On the other hand, if a clearly obscene book fails to incite a particular person to a criminal act, that is not in itself reason to prohibit censorship. For a single person of indomitable will and good training *does not dispatch a tendency;* we are after the curbing of the general incitements. That one person is not incited does not at all disprove that ten others might be. But even if there could not be shown *anyone* who had been incited, that still does not dispose of the case. For it may be that two books in conjunction are enough to incite where neither lying alone would be sufficient. There may be here, as in science, a certain "critical mass" beyond which crime follows. Certainly we have passed that "critical mass" long ago. We do not thereby advocate censorship, but by the same token neither do we advocate the cultivation of impure thoughts in young minds or in older minds unable to cope with them.

CHANGING MORALITY

Suppose, as it has sometimes been argued, that the purpose of a book is "to tear down and destroy generally accepted moral values as they exist." [1] This, it is argued, can be most effectively accomplished by a direct incitement, by a thoroughgoing piece of entertainment, not by a dry, scholarly presentation of a thoughtful philosophy.

Let us meet the issue head-on. Suppose that a book, in vivid scene after vivid scene, graphic description after same, portrays erotic actions to advance the idea that sex without love is not only permissible but good. The courts have often held that in our country we cannot ban a mere expression of ideas. Thus, to give the devil his due, it does not overcome the First Amendment argument to say of *Fanny Hill* that "the conclusions of some experts were pretty well strained in attempting to justify its claimed literary value: such as the book preached a moral that sex with is better than sex without love, when Fanny's descriptions of her sexual acts, particularly with the young boy she seduced, in Fanny's judgment at least, were to the contrary." [2] Suppose, that is, that the only idea advanced is that sex is fun and the grosser the sex the more the fun. Can

1. Quoting from Hallows, J., paraphrasing in dissent the characterization of *Tropic of Cancer* by a probation officer with a master's degree in social science, in *McCauley v. Tropic of Cancer*, 20 Wis. 2d 134, 121 N.W.2d 545 (1963).

2. *Memoirs v. Massachusetts*, 349 Mass. 69, 206 N.E.2d 403 (1965), upholding Finding 20 of trial court, quoted in *Memoirs*, 383 U.S. 413, 444 (1966).

such an idea be banned consistently with the First Amendment? In the words of one of our members, "You bet it can."

For the underlying moral basis of society is one which society may preserve. This power inheres in the notion of sovereignty. Free speech, Justice Holmes tells us, may be limited where there is a clear and present danger to an interest which the state has a legitimate reason to protect.[3] And it is on the consensus of a society, after all, that the entire superstructure of rules and laws and orderly procedures is based. For as the distinguished scholar Professor Robert A. Dahl has pointed out: "Prior to politics, beneath it, enveloping it, restricting it, conditioning it, is the underlying consensus on policy that usually exists in the society among a predominant portion of the politically active members." [4] There can be no serious quarrel with the proposition that a vastly predominant portion of our society is against the rampant spread of obscenity.

Businessmen, for instance, who are among the most tough-minded people in society, recently responded to a survey by *Nation's Business,* the journal of the Chamber of Commerce, concerning "action to raise morality minimums in print, on the air and on the screen." [5] In answer to the question, Should smut be curbed?, the affirmative reply topped the negative by a margin of ten to one. Thus, Foster G. McGaw, chairman of the American Hospital Supply Corporation of Evanston, Illinois, said, "Anything which undermines basic virtues should be outlawed. You can destroy our society by undercutting its respect for morality and integrity—and for our parents, grandparents, and forefathers." Likewise, J. C. Berghoff, the associate general counsel of Swift and Company, the meat marketers of Chicago, opined: "I do not take pen in hand to write to editors, frequently or even occasionally. But I feel strongly that one of our country's most serious problems of the day is the phe-

3. *Schenck v. United States,* 249 U.S. 47 (1919).
4. Dahl, *Preface to Democratic Theory* (Chicago: University of Chicago Press, 1956), p. 132.
5. See *Nation's Business,* December, 1969, pp. 20–21.

nomenon of rampant smut." And the vice-president of
Anchor Post Products, Inc., in Baltimore, C. John Gross,
notes that "smut disrupts the moral base of our civilized
society and tears asunder the cohesive family structure upon
which it depends." Recognizing that in America "everyone
speaks of 'freedom of speech' and 'freedom of the press,' "
Sam H. McLean of the McLean Insurance Agency in Athens,
Georgia, says that "there is another freedom they are for-
getting: 'freedom from filth.' "

These are only a sampling of the great outpouring of
opinions that flooded the editorial offices of *Nation's Business*. On another level, the mass burning of obscenity in
Philadelphia should not be overlooked. On September 29,
1963, in that city, more than five thousand pieces of pornography were burned before the chief of police, a large
audience, and a hymn-singing choir.[6] It should surprise no-
body that even Dr. Benjamin Spock, the prominent "leftist"
pediatrician, has recently endorsed the government's role in
controlling obscenity.[7]

It necessarily follows that society has the power to ward
off complete moral decay when that decay is advanced
through unlawful means.

Some would object on a purely pragmatic ground that
society will be ever precluded from "advancing" (or, at
least, changing) its morality if it cannot publish the new
kind of "morality" (read: immorality). That may be, as a
purely practical point, but by the same token if the por-
nographers *do* persuade society to change (through lawful
means) they will then have the community and the consensus with them, and we certainly do not advocate restrictions
on the right to vote!

We note, finally, that liberals and others have protested
the spread of firearms as tending to cause murder and other
crime. They do not want guns in the hands of perverts and
others. How then, we ask, can they advocate putting obscene

6. Noted by Earl F. Murphy, "The Value of Pornography," 10
Wayne Law Review 655, 677 (1964).
7. Dr. Benjamin Spock, *Decent and Indecent: Our Personal and
Political Behavior* (New York: McCall, 1970).

books in the hands of these same perverts and others? Guns kill, but so can pornography.[8]

THE COMMUNITY AFFECTED

Having decided on the general legal limits of censorship, it remains to isolate those classes or communities of people from whom obscenity can be lawfully withheld. The Supreme Court has said that even its own tests apply not to some artificial, pure community but to the "sexual interests" of the "intended and probable recipient group." [9] Thus a book cannot be said to be nonobscene because it fails to incite older men, or men of science, or political leaders. The question is what effect the allegedly obscene work will have on the group which will most likely get its hands on it.

First, the general public: In this day of mass marketing, many obscene books and pictures are circulated throughout the nation, intended to reach high and low into every local community, and within reach of literally everyone. The problem is, of course, that there are so many diverse interests and predilections in the general public that it would be difficult to sense out all the possibly obscene matter. While some of it would clearly be offensive to everyone, or at least to enough to extract a group consensus, there might be some material that would not in fact be offensive to everyone but would in fact be highly inflammable in the hands of localized and restricted groups within the general community. It is also true that in the hands of mature adults, much material that would inflame these localized groups would have no criminal effect. So a general censorship as to everyone is too sweeping.

Second, localized groups: There are certain more restricted classes of people to whom the tests of obscenity can be applied, however. Most important of these are children

8. See Part II. Of course, since it is outside our jurisdiction, we express no opinion on the merits of gun control legislation.
9. *Mishkin v. New York*, 383 U.S. 502, 509 (1966).

and women; and here we find an unexpected result of the general theory that that which can be censored is that which will tend to incite a criminal response. For while it is clear that the immature, still-forming minds of children can be drastically affected and harmed by the debilitating influence of obscenity, it is not so clear that the mature woman can be.

CHILDREN

The clearest case for censorship is that of children. They who are susceptible to the subtle and not-so-subtle suggestions and hints of vivid obscenity cannot, almost by definition, protect themselves. Once read, obscenity has worked its harm. No amount of pure reading thereafter can undo that harm. Not until the young mind is prepared and educated can it withstand the assaults of vile but tempting suggestiveness. It is precisely because children are young and defenseless that obscenity works its evil, and it is precisely for this reason, also, that community protection in the form of censorship is most desirable.

It should be clear, therefore, that censorship of obscenity and pornography which is intended to reach children does not fall within the proscriptions of the First Amendment and can constitutionally be sustained. To deny this proposition is to deny any possibility of censorship whatsoever, insofar as it relates to obscenity. We think the evidence abundantly supports the policy of restricting the flow of pornography to minors, and we conclude, therefore, that it is within the permissible limits of censorship to make illegal the sale of obscene matter to minors.

WOMEN

A different aspect is presented in the case of adult women (and even, possibly, mature young women). Women are generally incapable of rape and only rarely have they been involved in crimes of sexual molestations; at least, they have not been involved to anything like the extent men have. Furthermore, there is evidence to suggest that when it comes to obscenity women are far less susceptible, for some reason, than are men; perhaps it is the more wholesome conditioning society gives to women at an early age; perhaps it is due to a more fundamental natural cause.[10] But where there is less possibility that women will be incited and where there is less reason to believe that they will commit crimes there is less reason to restrict the flow of obscenity to them, at least on a strict reading of the general theory of the limits of censorship as it pertains to obscenity. This will be received as an unexpected conclusion.

There is, however, another aspect to be considered. The typical American housewife is not likely to be affected by the average pornographic novel. But her children clearly might be, and although she might not have pornography on her bookshelves because she finds it disgusting, her children might nevertheless find it next door at the home of their playmates whose mother might be unable to prevent their father from buying and keeping it. If we permit adults (even women) to possess it, children will inevitably get it, possibly even from next door. If we wish to attack the evil, therefore, we must ban all obscenity and prevent not merely children, but adults as well, from having it within their possession. Thus we are led into a quandary, because we have seen at the outset that we can censor only if the tendency to incitement is present, and we have seen that it is not present as to mature adults.

The answer is not entirely free from doubt. But surely,

10. See Kinsey, *Sexual Behavior in the Human Female* (Philadelphia: Saunders, 1953), Chapter 16.

if it is to be a national goal to restrict the flow of obscenity to minors, it seems clear that enforcement activities and officials must bear the major brunt of the restriction program. Not only must direct sales to minors be prohibited, but also sanctions must be imposed on those who give, or cause to be given, obscenity to minors. To these specific control mechanisms we next turn.

PART IV

RECOMMENDATIONS

Section 1: Partisanship and Pornography

NOTHING CAN UNDERMINE a useful—even necessary—federal program more quickly than to make a partisan, political issue out of it. We wish to emphasize emphatically that critical to the success of whatever program is eventually adopted is that it be nonpartisan and nonpolitical. To do this it is necessary to recognize that opponents of government control of the obscene are, for the most part, entirely sincere. It would be a great mistake not to realize this. In order to establish a successful federal obscenity program we must be prepared to believe that liberals do not just shout "free speech" as an issue: They actually believe in it.

Thus it will not do to argue that Justice William O. Douglas is merely being snide when he uses language such as this in an obscenity opinion: "But the Commonwealth of Massachusetts instituted the suit [against the book *Fanny Hill*] that ultimately found its way here, praying that the book be declared obscene so that the citizens of Massachusetts might be spared the necessity of determining for themselves whether or not to read it." [1] Justice Douglas, and many others, no doubt sincerely believe that citizens should be afforded the opportunity to decide whether a book is obscene. In our view, Justice Douglas misses the point, for it is not so much a question of the right of the individual to decide whether a book is pornographic as it is a question of

1. *Memoirs v. Massachusetts*, opinion of Mr. Justice Douglas, 383 U.S. 413, 426 (1966).

the right of the majority of the people to decide *through their government* the same issue. This is not an argument for a welfare state. Far from it. But pornography is so insidious that it can wend its way into even the purest homes. Indeed, in the case of advertising, it does so nightly. Nor does it save the day to concede we know obscenity when we see it, for though we may know heroin when we see it, it nevertheless is used.

But all this notwithstanding, no federal program will be made secure by questioning the motives or sincerity of Justice Douglas and others. They must be educated to the dangers, but in a nonpartisan way. Only if the opposition sees that those who would control obscenity are men of goodwill and magnanimity will reason ultimately prevail.

Section 2: Law Enforcement

THE REALM OF law enforcement provides a wealth of opportunities for combating the existence and flow of obscenity.

It is highly questionable whether the federal government has adequately assumed the full burden of national leadership in dealing with problems of obscenity. States and municipalities are groping valiantly but futilely for advice on how best to fight the menace, looking in vain for funds needed to implement promising new programs, and despairing of finding the trained and experienced personnel who might lead new efforts in the battle.

The federal government can help mostly with money, men, and minds. Technical assistance teams could be formed at the national level to help localities devise programs and legislation most responsive to pornography problems in a given area. The teams could be made available for assistance to any section of the country, only upon request of that section, thereby preventing the specter of a national police force. Federal funds would be used to recruit team members, effectively allowing states and localities to get something for nothing upon request. Dissemination of existing knowledge concerning obscenity could thus be maximized, and enforcement officials from every section of the country would be able to examine pornography samples from other sections. In such a manner, the collective specialized expertise of all would be nurtured and developed.

To emphasize to the nation this Administration's concern about and dedication to the problem of obscenity, consideration should be given to the creation of a new high-level position within the Administration, perhaps with a designation of Special Assistant to the President. Selection of a man of indisputably high national stature and unimpeachable moral integrity would prove this Administration's deep commitment to the problem. Although the official need not have Cabinet status, the new commitment would be highlighted by allowing him to report directly to the President. The President's Task Force on Executive Reorganization could more formally designate the relationship between that official and the administrative agency discussed below (pp. 114-116).

The Task Force also endorses utilization of federal Strike Forces to coordinate the present level of federal involvement in the fight against obscenity. These Forces would function under the aegis of the newly appointed official described above. Supervisory personnel including Justice Department attorneys, FBI investigatory agents, customs officials, IRS agents, and the like would gather periodically to isolate those areas of the country deemed most dangerously engrossed in obscenity. Enforcement teams would then be dispatched to the selected areas in a cohesive federal unit to work with local officials. Such a coordinated effort would maximize the dissemination of needed intelligence, prevent duplication of effort, and concentrate enforcement resources where the need is greatest. Where necessary to the national security, such teams could apply as a unit for judicial authorization of telephone wire taps upon a showing of clear and present danger of use of interstate communication facilities for dissemination of obscenity. To best isolate the areas whose need for such coordinated federal assistance is greatest, the Task Force endorses the concept of a permanent Presidential Task Force on Obscenity Statistics which would meet periodically to collate all available data on obscenity trends nationwide and, when necessary, order research to clarify ambiguous areas.

Although the realm of organizational structure provides fertile ground for planting the seeds of the destruction of obscenity, other areas equally favorable to the task exist. Perhaps no field could be mined as profitably as that of the enforcement field itself.

Police departments throughout the country are undermanned, underpaid, underequipped, and undereducated for the difficult problems of enforcement of anti-obscenity laws. As one "unintellectual" but perceptive deputy sheriff in rural Oklahoma told a staff member, "You've gotta nab'm before you can give'm their civil rights." Yet limitations of present-day enforcement personnel and techniques pose serious obstacles to "nabbing'm."

Many studies have indicated that the ability of police to arrest a suspect depends significantly on the speed with which they can respond to a citizen's distress call. Yet police chiefs from every metropolitan area lament the fact that response time to reports of obscenity violations far exceeds a tolerable level because of crowded police radio frequencies. To aid in the apprehension of violators, therefore, the Task Force recommends that the Attorney General, Secretary of Defense, and Secretary of Commerce, in conjunction with the Federal Communications Commission, study and recommend a re-allocation of radio frequencies.

Even when police do arrive promptly at the scene of reported obscenity offenses, very often the suspect is in flight. With the unsophisticated weaponry to which most police today are limited, the officer is confronted with only two alternative courses of action: shoot, or watch an offender escape. Obvious problems of morality and of community relations would flow, in most cases, from the officer shooting a suspect under those circumstances. Yet the alternative of allowing the offender to get away scot-free is not itself a satisfactory resolution. The Task Force therefore recommends federal funding of research designed to develop nonlethal weapons as a viable alternative to the present disturbing dilemma.

The present inadequacy of police response generally to problems of pornography could be improved by several other innovations, many of which should be encouraged by federal expenditures. In order to develop and train obscenity enforcement personnel in the intricacies of their specialization, considerably higher levels of education are necessary. Such education could be provided by federal assurance of sharing, on an equal basis, the costs of graduate and, when necessary, postgraduate education. After all, indecencies contain their own subtleties; would the public tolerate unskilled laborers' performing neurosurgery? As a further spur to local efforts, the federal government should help finance metropolitan planning among local obscenity enforcement agencies. Such planning would most fruitfully allow utilization of the expertise of all available specialists and would encourage, through action grants and otherwise, the establishment of specialty obscenity squads to wipe filth from the most dangerous obscenity haunts of each locality. The establishment of such cross-local development might best be accomplished by administrative fiat declaring such development a prerequisite for funding under the Model Cities Program.[1]

It would be dangerously inaccurate to assume, however, that obscenity should be fought strictly at the police level. As we have noted earlier, billions of units of obscenity are imported annually into this country. The borders, therefore, provide an ideal site to concentrate enforcement personnel. Despite the obviousness of this target, resources allocated to these areas have traditionally been painfully inadequate. Typically, in fiscal 1960, the United States Bureau of Customs in Boston opened only 5 percent of some 43 million packages. As the Deputy Collector of Customs has reported, "[I]f we had more men to open more packages, we would get more of this filth." [2] The Task Force recommends that the Department of Labor assign its Division of Manpower to determine the manpower needs of an effective customs

1. Governmental zeal in combating obscenity, rather than "impinging on the First Amendment," actually prevents resort to self-help by the decent if silent majority. In England, for example, such is not the case. Only recently, the wife of a top British newspaper executive was kidnapped and her life threatened unless her husband's newspaper "stop printing filth." *Washington Evening Star*, January 2, 1970, p. A3.

2. Hearings, p. 238.

screening for obscenity, and that the federal government expand the present level of its customs force to accommodate that finding.

Even at its present level, the Bureau of Customs can strike an immediate blow at the smut business in America. The Department of Justice has learned that the famous Kronhausen exhibit, consisting of erotic art by so-called renowned artists, will shortly be shipped from Europe to Baltimore. The Task Force recommends that the Administration show its resoluteness now, in an unequivocal manner, by seizing that cargo or instituting court proceedings to enjoin importation or exhibition of those works on our shores.

There is, of course, a limit to the potential effectiveness of men and money as tools of enforcement, a limit which the federal government seems occasionally to have overlooked. It is unrealistic to suppose that even the most effective customs effort will totally eliminate illegal importation of obscenity into this country. The Task Force recommends, therefore, that appreciable diplomatic attention be directed toward persuading those countries which, through the legalization of obscenity, provide the major foreign supply of obscenity, to revise their own obscenity laws. Such an effort, whatever its likely cost, would undeniably be less expensive and more productive in curtailing the flow of foreign obscenity into this country than simply increasing the number of customs officials.

In addition to these generalized approaches toward the elimination of obscenity, specific legislation is also in order. These proposals do not require detailed explanation. Human sympathy no less than practical criminological insight dictates that the seller of obscenity, both the neighborhood pusher and his supplier, should be treated more severely than the unfortunate user. By removing the cornerstone, the house will topple. The Task Force therefore recommends passage of an immunity statute which would allow the Attorney General or his designated representative to compel Grand Jury testimony from any individual who he has probable cause to believe can provide information helpful in convicting the Mr. Big of obscenity. Refusal to so testify would subject the individual to citation for contempt of court.

Even those offenders whom the present system has been able to apprehend, however, have been dealt with improperly. Correctional and probation departments assigned to obscenity cases are generally understaffed, undertrained and, often, sexually immature themselves. To rectify this sorry picture, the Task Force recommends establishment of a national scholarship program to encourage bright young men and women to pursue study and training in the area of obscenity corrections. The program could be modeled after the present White House Fellows Program, with selected members undergoing a thorough educational experience under the tutelage of experienced men totally familiar with the problems of rehabilitating obscenity offenders.

Innovative correctional techniques for dealing with obscenity violators should also be considered. Social scientists and concerned public officials are all too familiar with the unhealthy conditions of so many of today's penal institutions, and the debilitating effect those conditions can exert on prisoners.[3] The Task Force therefore recommends that the Federal Bureau of Prisons formulate guidelines to assist prison authorities, federal and local, in expanding usage of work-release programs and halfway houses in dealing with obscenity offenders. Such programs, properly regulated and supervised, would increase markedly the success of the obscenity violator's subsequent release and integration into the community. America cannot afford a system of criminal justice amounting to little more than revolving doors for obscenity recidivists.

At the same time, we ought never to lose sight of the fact that these obscenity violators, however innocent their intentions, have in fact violated the law. And it is clear that people are less likely to violate the law if they can be reasonably sure they will be subjected to punishment as a

---

3. See *Crime Commission Report: Task Force Report on Corrections.*

consequence.[4] It is not with lack of insight that J. Edgar Hoover himself, Director of the FBI, has argued that increased punishments deter obscenity violations.[5] Such an argument persuasively answers those who hold that government cannot legislate morality. It seems beyond argument, for example, that entrepreneurs recently convicted for mailing five copies of *Sex Life of a Cop* and sentenced to twenty-five years' imprisonment will not be selling pornography for quite some time.[6] The Task Force therefore recommends that the President ask Congress to broaden the mandate given its Commission on Revision of Federal Criminal Laws to reevaluate the present sentencing policies of the United States Code with an eye toward possible increases in obscenity sentences. The concepts of mandatory minimum sentences for sales to minors and preventive detention for a period not to exceed six months for repeat offenders should also be fully explored.

But police and corrections do not exhaust the spectrum of enforcement efforts. The actual prosecution of obscenity offenses offers the federal government perhaps its most glittering opportunity for striking effective blows at obscenity traffic. The Task Force endorses, as a bipartisan measure, a program suggested in recent years by Representative John Dowdy (D. Tex.).[7] Obscenity violators should be given fully to understand that, although they may have support for their minority philosophy in the majority philosophy of Supreme Court opinions, the forces of decency, law, and order do not lack resources. The Supreme Court may have declared unconstitutional the sending of smut peddlers to jail, but they have not yet condemned taking them to court. The Task Force recommends a stepped-up

4. See, for example, Johs Andenaes, "General Prevention—Illusion or Reality?" 43 *Journal of Criminal Law, Criminology and Police Science*, No. 2.

5. Address of J. Edgar Hoover at the National Convention of the American Legion, September 19, 1957.

6. *United States v. West Coast News Company et al.*, 357 F.2d 855 (6th Cir. 1966).

7. Reported in 2 *Law In Transition Quarterly* 97 (1967).

program of obscenity prosecutions across the country. The courts may ultimately throw protective covering around nudie magazines and sordid books, but the cost of purchasing that protection can be made so prohibitive as to send the publishers to a different business to make a faster buck.

Federal sponsorship of these programs, and their development and implementation by municipal authorities, will certainly cost money; but as the old saw has it, you get what you pay for. America may very well not have sufficient economic flexibility to implement an effective broad-range program of obscenity control while at the same time engaging in war in Vietnam. If so, the Administration will simply have to redefine its national priorities. Surely the threat to our internal security posed by the flood of obscenity is worthy of considerable fiscal expenditure, whatever the effects may be on our success in a faraway war. America must learn that she cannot both have her cake and eat it too.

Section 3: An Administrative Solution

THE DIRKSEN IDEA

Throughout the many long years that he held national public office, Senator Everett McKinley Dirksen espoused strict control and regulation of obscenity. Shortly before he died, Senator Dirksen formulated a plan that he thought would be remarkably effective in reducing the flow of pornography.[1] In essence, Senator Dirksen proposed that local juries be made the final arbiters of community standards. By removing jurisdiction from the courts to define community standards as a matter of law, the local jury, the one group most intimately in contact with community standards, could assess each allegedly obscene book, film, play, or picture on the factual merits. Does the book or other material affront contemporary community standards? The jury, drawn from that community, would perform in fact what it has always performed in theory: the safeguarding of community moral standards.

Senator Dirksen argued that to empower local juries with such authority would reduce smut *because* the jury would inevitably apply contemporary standards and come out against obviously obscene material. We think that Senator Dirksen erred as to the causal relationship; we support

1. See, for example, his article in *Reader's Digest*, November, 1969.

Senator Dirksen's plan nevertheless, for the reasons immediately following.

The problem, as we have already seen, is that local community standards are far too lax. Pornography does not flourish simply because of unscrupulous and immoral purveyors; it flourishes fundamentally because people read it. For instance, even in rural communities, filthy motion pictures are patronized by the majority of inhabitants. Tests have shown that when local theaters substitute general family movies for the so-called adult fare they had been serving, patronage declines markedly.[2] It is from this very class of pornography consumers, therefore, that Senator Dirksen's local juries would be drawn. Were they to apply local community standards—as reflected in what most people in the community seem to want—we might well expect to find an increase, rather than a decrease, in the amount of allowable obscenity. For this reason, we conclude that Senator Dirksen did err.

However, we do not believe that this error is fatal to the case Senator Dirksen put forward. Quite the contrary, we consider the local jury indispensable to the solution of the problem.

For the genius of the local jury is that it does *not* apply the local community standard as reflected in the actual behavior of the people. Rather, the local jury applies the *expected* or *anticipated moral standard*. This anticipated moral standard is that which each member of the jury thinks other members of the jury expect him to possess. Thus, when a prosecutor presents a piece of smut to the jury for consideration, it would be highly unlikely that, presented with material so characterized by the prosecutor, the jury would ever decide to the contrary; it is simply unlikely that any man or woman in the jury room would be brazen enough to suggest that his moral standards are so lax that

2. The community reaction to such a policy in St. Mary's County, Maryland, a rural county, during 1969 was precisely this. See the St. Mary's *Enterprise*, the weekly newspaper of Leonardtown, Maryland, during spring, 1969.

he would permit himself or his children to read or look at smut, the actual fact notwithstanding.

We conclude, therefore, that Senator Dirksen's sound instincts led him to suggest an alluring solution to the general problem of obscenity. We conclude, further, that enabling legislation which puts the local-jury plan into effect would be a fitting testimonial to the memory of the distinguished Senator. We therefore recommend that local juries be made the final arbiters of community standards in the evaluation of obscene material from whatever source.

For the sake of simplicity in the discussion that follows, we shall refer to this recommendation as "the Dirksen idea." Its implementation would actually be quite simple. Congress and the state legislatures, as a general matter, have plenary power over the jurisdiction of the federal and state court systems. It would be neither unconstitutional nor difficult to enact laws curbing the jurisdiction of federal and state courts in the area of obscenity to this degree: The courts would not have jurisdiction to consider the factual merits of individual cases brought under the general obscenity laws. This question—obviously the critical question in any obscenity trial—would be left entirely in the hands of the jury and could not be reviewed by any court. Thus, whether or not a book, for example, was an affront to contemporary community standards and so forth would be beyond the reach of judges. By simply limiting judicial jurisdiction, we need not enter into the complicated problem of censorship.[3]

---

3. Since the jury is to be selected from the local community, where there may reside some people who would themselves like to read obscene books and watch dirty movies, every effort must be made by prosecutors to ensure that this type of prospective juror is not empaneled. Prosecuting attorneys must be careful to elicit on *voir dire* what their opinions are. A juror with a short skirt should be challenged. This is done now in capital cases when a potential juror confesses that he is opposed to the death penalty. The same principle should be extended to obscenity trials; doubtless, other techniques can be devised to secure a more impartial trial of the issues.

THE FEDERAL COURT
OF OBSCENITY APPEALS

Of course, it is a truism that juries can sometimes be led astray by emotion and passion. The very fact that the jury is applying a community standard which none of the individual jurors in their private capacity may actually adhere to, supports the proposition that the local jury may occasionally err. Sometimes, that is, a book or movie which attempts to discuss honest sex in a realistic way may be mistaken as one which goes beyond the permissibly erotic.

For that reason, some route of appeal should be established. Inherent in our democratic system is the possibility of appealing any decision, no matter how democratically or openly arrived at. In the past, however, as we have seen, appeal to the courts has simply opened the doors to a flood of pornography itself. For that reason we recommended the jury be made the final arbiter of community standards. The appellate agency, therefore, should not be one of the presently constituted courts of record in the United States.

We recommend, therefore, the establishment of a new federal court, to have final appellate jurisdiction in the sole area of obscenity.

For convenience, we here term that court the Federal Court of Obscenity Appeals. To insulate the judges from political pressure, we recommend that the judges of this court be appointed for life terms during good behavior. We recommend further that a panel of judges—perhaps seven or nine—be appointed to hear all appeals *en banc*. Since this would be a court in all respects the same as other federal courts save only its limited jurisdiction, it should be subject to the same rules and procedures, especially since this would greatly ease the burden of those lawyers who would have to practice before it.

We hasten to point out that the establishment of such a court would not be to reintroduce *sub rosa* judicial standards in the factual determination. For the Federal Court of

Obscenity Appeals would be limited in hearing only questions of law. Thus, while it could decide whether or not a book as a matter of law could be classed as beyond the contemporary community standard, it could not determine whether or not the book was in fact an affront to contemporary community standards or whether or not the book in fact was obscene. Thus, again, the issue of censorship would be avoided, and in two ways. Not only would this new court be barred from censoring, but the limitation on the Supreme Court's appellate jurisdiction would have the effect of taking from that court the duty of deciding such appeals, thus obviating the unhealthy possibility that that court might someday itself be forced to be an agency of censorship. For the Supreme Court, no less than any other agency of government, should not be put in a situation where it might someday be compelled to render such a decision.

In this, we find support from a surprising quarter. For more than a quarter of a century, Justice Hugo Black has been opposed to any form of government censorship and has therefore uniformly dissented in cases in which the government has sought to ban obscene material. Yet even Justice Black has recently said: "I believe the tedious, time-consuming and unwelcome responsibility for finally deciding what particular discussions or opinions must be suppressed in this country, should, for the good of this Court and of the nation, be vested in some governmental institution or institutions other than this Court." [4] We agree.

THE FEDERAL OBSCENITY
AND PORNOGRAPHY BOARD

In view of the extremely serious influx of pornographic material into the United States during the last decade, we have sought a broader solution than the mere suppression of the known circulating mass. When a seller is actually

4. Black, J., dissenting, in *Mishkin v. New York*, 383 U.S. 502, 516–517 (1966).

caught, he can of course be prosecuted. But the processes of the criminal law are slow—due process and fair trials, unfortunately, take time. In our view, there is little time left.

Consequently, we have considered the possibility of a more general administrative solution to the problem of obscenity in America. Just as independent federal agencies have been created during the last seventy-five years to deal with a host of specific problems in which the expertise of trained and experienced administrators can do much to regulate and control an industry, so we have concluded, after much discussion, that the establishment of a federal agency devoted to the regulation of obscene matter would be a highly beneficial means to police and control the area.

We recommend, therefore, that a Federal obscenity and Pornography Board be created, subject to the general Federal Administrative Law, to regulate and control the flow of obscene and pornographic matter in the United States.

The advantages of such a Federal Obscenity and Pornography Board (FOPB) should be obvious. First, because the Board would be administrative, it could be delegated rule-making authority to deal with the countless unforeseeable problems that occur in the policing of any industry. Secondly, the expertise of such a Board would develop over time; and under enabling legislation, it would have a continuing writ to investigate, issue subpoenas, and hold inquiries into the entire field, all of which actions courts could not undertake. By combining both these possibilities, the Board would be uniquely situated to develop and administer a national obscenity policy.

Thus, as an example of one kind of novel solution the FOPB might develop, we have investigated the possibility of compulsory federal registration of pornography readers. Since the danger inherent in pornography is its impact on the reader, who will in all likelihood be tempted to commit crime, it might be a necessary part of a broad national policy of control to impose sanctions on readers, as well as on sellers. Reader registration would achieve this objective. Anyone found to have been reading literature (or watching movies, and so on) determined beforehand by local juries to be pornographic or obscene would be compelled to register as a reader of pornography. No criminal penalty would attach as a registrant (though there would be criminal penalties for failure to register). No social stigma would be attached either, for the FOPB would presumably strictly maintain its list under the general exceptions to the Freedom of Information Act, 5 U.S.C. §552(b), and under general implementing legislation to be enacted. But the Board would know who was reading pornographic literature, and this would greatly simplify its tasks in investigation of sellers (as it would likewise simplify the problem of law-enforcement bureaus, which would be empowered to seek the help of FOPB when certain crimes had been committed).

The FOPB would also have adjudicatory functions to perform, much as the National Labor Relations Board must decide cases between unions and employers and the Federal Communications Commission must decide between disputing license applicants. Trial examiners would be empowered under rules to be promulgated in the Federal Register to hear cases and to recommend to the Board actions to be taken. Thus the decision as to whether a particular person should be compelled to register as a reader of pornography might be left as an initial matter to the trial examiner. Inasmuch as such a case would be civil, not criminal, in nature, the rules of procedure could be greatly simplified to bring about a speedier resolution of the issues and a far swifter implementation of federal obscenity policy.

Agencies are not unerring providers of federal policy, of course. It goes without saying that the FOPB could reach beyond its delegated power when promulgating rules, could decide cases not in accord with its statutory authority, and could even use its authority as a cover to harass and intimidate persons who were within their legal rights in refusing to answer questions propounded by the Board. Some avenue of appeal would doubtless be necessary.

We conclude that appeal should be to the Federal Court of Obscenity Appeals, rather than to the federal courts of appeal, as is the usual case. Since we are dealing with a particular and unique problem, it seems wise to direct

appeals from the one agency uniquely qualified to develop
policy to the one court uniquely qualified to pass on it. In
this way, the constitutional rights of litigants, registrants,
and others could be safeguarded; in this way, too, the
motives and methods of the FOPB would be far less open
to question. For where decisions of a federal agency can
be spread on the record of a reviewing court and be merci-
lessly exposed to the harsh light of public opinion, the
governmental institution will adhere to its mandate, and
public confidence in the functioning of government will be
preserved and maintained.

THE MAKING OF
NATIONAL OBSCENITY POLICY

The Task Force at one time considered whether specific
legislation ought to be enacted spelling out in detail what
types of writing, art, and movies ought to be within the
general proscription against obscenity. The legislation considered was to have been a lengthy code, so comprehensive
that it would even enumerate what words could and could
not be used in conjunction with each other within the
general pornographic frame. On reconsideration, the idea
was scotched.

The task was too large for legislation. Inevitably, there
would be a word missing here or there which a purveyor or
other person would attempt to take advantage of at a prosecution or other hearing. Besides, part of the genius of the
American people has been our ability to avoid legal codes
such as are used in the continental legal systems in Europe.
Consequently, it was decided that the Federal Obscenity
and Pornography Board could perform the tasks implicitly
performed in the drafting of a mature code. Since there
would likely be heated argument about the particulars of
any specific code, it would be unlikely that Congress would
take speedy or decisive action on the particulars. But a
federal administrative agency can take action which a

balky Congress would want to sidestep. The federal administrative agency can take these steps on a case-by-case
basis, defining and considering the specifics step by step as
they arise. Thus, to cite only one of many possible examples,
the FOPB could perform the continuing function of deciding which words could legitimately be used in scientific
works, popular nonfiction, and fictional work. To take a
simple case, FOPB would undoubtedly ban such words as
"f-ck" or "c-nt" in fiction at the outset. The use of other
words, such as "penis" and "copulation," more likely depends on the context in which they were set, and the
definitive treatise on their use could only be written after
sufficient cases came to the FOPB to discern the numerous
possibilities present. Thus the law could grow to meet the
national needs.

RECHANNELING OBSCENITY AND PORNOGRAPHY

Throughout the entire preceding discussion, the relevance
of the historic origins of pornography and obscenity has
perhaps been insufficiently emphasized. At a time when
literacy was small, pornography and general obscenity were
not widespread. History teaches that only as pornography
spreads to a greater part of the population have civiliza-
tions decayed and collapsed. When only small parts of the
upper class in Rome had access to the rare pornographic
work of the time, the danger was small. The Roman Empire
collapsed only after these works, and generally debilitating
activity, spread to larger and larger segments of the
population.

Nowhere throughout history, however, has it been suggested that the mere possession of obscenity, in and of
itself, can cause the collapse of civilization. Leaders in all
nations have never been accused of being any the less
capable to govern the affairs of their nations by virtue of
whatever collections of pornography, be it paintings or
books, the national galleries and archives have possessed.

Quite the contrary, the historical evidence strongly suggests that pornography, when it is in the hands of that class of people who, because of their upbringing and training, can tolerate it, does not produce harmful effects on the general population, nor in the dealings of that class among itself. That is, those sufficiently educated—with a sufficient amount of what was once termed "breeding"—are unlikely to be affected by whatever might pass among the general populace as obscenity.

Thus, as a leading monograph on the subject has noted:

> It has been held that books such as Payne's edition of the *Arabian Nights,* Fielding's novel *Tom Jones,* the works of Rabelais, Ovid's *Art of Love,* the *Decameron of Bocaccio,* the *Heptameron of Queen Margaret of Navarre,* and *Aladdin* are not obscene, this conclusion being reached upon the theories that these works are the product of great literary genius, that they rank with the higher literature and *are not generally purchased or appreciated by the class of people from whom unclean publications should be withheld,* and that such books are not corrupting in their influence upon the young because they are not likely to reach them.[5]

While we realize that it is currently unfashionable to speak of elites or "Establishments," we strongly urge that the President and Congress give due consideration to the factors above elucidated. Undoubtedly this is another area in which federal administrative policy could be of enormous benefit: By rechanneling the distribution and consumption of whatever level of obscenity must necessarily be produced to those who can absorb it without harm, the problems of pornography and obscenity will be largely solved. Especially is this true should obscenity be available to all adults.

The general conclusion is inescapable. Federal policy in the area of obscenity and pornography is greatly in need of coordination and breadth. These can be most efficiently accomplished by the establishment of a federal agency to

5. 33 *American Jurisprudence* 21–22; emphasis added.

deal with national problems, by the institution of local jury fact-finding in obscenity cases, and by the establishment of the seven- or nine-member Federal Court of Obscenity Appeals to make final rulings in the area of constitutional regulation of the interstate flow of obscenity and pornography.

Section 4: The Root Causes

IT IS SOMETIMES SAID—and then not inaccurately—that an ounce of prevention is worth a pound of cure. Such must assuredly be the case in the battle against obscenity. Especially with the prohibitive costs of the cures detailed earlier, the country should give very real consideration to attacking the problem at its roots rather than at its twigs.

The Task Force recommends a two-pronged attack at the roots of obscenity.

EDUCATION

In the first instance, the Task Force recommends a concentrated program aimed at educating the public to the dangers, inherent and resultant, of consumption of obscenity. Clever advertising, and its huge costs, would be unnecessary to such a program. The truth, the facts, the data which shroud obscenity in a shadow of undesirability are persuasive argument by themselves for the demise both of obscenity consumption generally and resort to obscenity in particular cases. We must and can persuade with logic, not gimmickry.

If logic and facts are the nuts and bolts of such persuasion, there is no lack for hammers and anvils. The lessons of virtue can be preached not only in the churches, but in the schools. We do not recommend, of course, that the Administration attempt to influence various religious groups to follow specific teaching programs and methods in educating their parishioners to the evils of obscenity. Such a policy would present serious constitutional issues concerning the proper demarcation between church and state; furthermore, it is largely unnecessary, in view of the splendid job America's churches are doing in the realm of morality. Without fostering the growth of any particular denomination, however, the Administration should consider sharing ratably the cost of such church-sponsored educational ventures.

America's schools, on the other hand, provide ideal tablets on which to carve the new morality. At our advanced stage of understanding of the processes of human mental development, it would be folly to gainsay the fact that children are impressionable, and that their early impressions often form the mold into which their adult personalities are poured. Encouragement by the federal government of worthwhile educational enterprises by dangling the carrot of financial support is hardly a new concept; witness most recently the highly praised Civil Rights Act of 1965. The Task Force recommends that this concept of selective federal funding be broadened by empowering the Department of Health, Education and Welfare to grant and withhold such funds as it deems necessary to assure appropriate attention by educational institutions to the problems of obscenity.

Naturally, however, these same children, no matter how thoroughly schooled during the day to the dangers of obscenity, return at night to their homes and, ultimately, to their television sets. Any involvement by the federal government in the arena of free communication is one to be avoided as a rule of thumb, for constitutional as well as practical philosophical reasons.[1] Yet the mere status of being a government should not strip the government of the rights afforded every individual citizen. There would seem, therefore, no reason in either law or logic to prevent the

1. See p. 37 ff.

federal government from presenting its message through the same privately controlled media used by private enterprises for advertising purposes. The government could thus present its case over those same airwaves which permit, if not encourage, that "moral pollution" so eloquently stripped bare by Senator McClellan.

> I invite concerned parents and all Americans who value decency and reject cultural decadence to raise their voice in protest against the possibility of the airwaves being polluted. We talk frequently about air pollution but . . . "moral" pollution is a considerably greater danger to this Nation.[2]

The war against moral pollution could be waged alongside the decade-long war against other environmental pollution promised by the President on the occasion of his signing the National Environmental Policy Act of 1969.

Even this, however, would not exhaust the media through which obscenity spreads. The Task Force recommends that the Administration in effect "bite the bullet" by using obscene literature itself as an educational vehicle. The Federal Obscenity and Pornography Board would certify certain literature on the borderline of obscenity which could not fairly or legally be censored, and would require that the publishers of that "literature" affix thereto the warning that obscenity can be hazardous both to the individual and to society. Such a warning is justified by the data of which this Task Force is aware. If there is any doubt, the Board could authorize funds for independent study by the Surgeon General to validate the point scientifically. This Administration itself has recently announced that in the year since similar warnings have been affixed to cigarette packages, American cigarette consumption has declined by over one billion cigarettes.[3] A similar advance in curtailing obscenity consumption would be a milestone.

2. *Congressional Record*, September, 22, 1969, p. 11035.
3. *The New York Times*, December 23, 1969, p. 27.

THE AMERICAN DREAM

Important as educational techniques loom in the fight against obscenity, improvements at the very sources of the problem represent equally significant opportunities to eliminate obscenity.

As we have noted earlier,[4] the reasons behind many Americans' resort to obscenity are varied and complex. The battle should be fought on the battlefield of those reasons. Consumption of obscenity is really a symptom of social ills that have become endemic in our society.

We do not claim competence to chart the details of programs within such complex and interrelated fields as employment, welfare, and housing. We do believe it is essential to set forth goals and to recommend strategies to reach those goals.

Much has been accomplished in recent years to formulate new directions for national policy and new channels for national emergency. Resources devoted to social programs have been greatly increased in many areas. Hence, few of our program suggestions are entirely novel. In some form, many are already in effect.

Unemployment and underemployment are among the persistent and serious grievances of disadvantaged minorities. The pervasive effect of these conditions on the inner cities especially is inextricably linked to the problem of obscenity. Hence, the Task Force recommends continued emphasis on national economic growth and job creation to assure jobs for those newly trained without displacing those already satisfactorily employed.

The federal government should also initiate programs offering concentrated job training by both public and private employers while at the same time dispensing information regarding available jobs, training, and supportive aids. To break the unemployment cycle of despair which drives

4. See p. 54 ff.

so many Americans to obscenity, such programs should also stimulate public and private investment in depressed urban and rural areas, with an eye toward broadening the ladder of social mobility.

The Task Force also believes that our present system of public assistance contributes materially to the tensions and social disorganization that breed the market for obscenity. It excludes large numbers of persons who are in great need, while providing, for those whom it does assist, funds well below the minimum necessary for a decent level of existence such as might encourage productivity and self-sufficiency. Small wonder such people turn to obscenity for whatever false comfort it provides.

The current Administration has recently persuaded a reluctant Congress to pass, at last, a welfare program which may in practice, as it does in principle, alleviate those shortcomings. The Task Force suggests several measures to assure that the new system does not perpetuate that sharp bitterness between givers and recipients by daily reminding recipients that they are considered untrustworthy, ungrateful, promiscuous, and lazy—for with such a self-image, one who turns for warmth to obscenity cannot genuinely be faulted.

The Task Force therefore recommends that welfare systems throughout the country be administered in such a fashion as to provide more adequate standards of assistance on the basis of uniform national standards; that such standards be reviewed periodically by the Secretary of HEW to prevent reliance upon outdated standards; and that in the day-to-day doling-out process of the system, welfare workers be trained to conceal whatever attitudes they may have about what seems, to them as workers, the shiftless attitudes of their clients. For we are often what we think ourselves to be; and if a class of people are encouraged to think themselves dirty, so will they turn to dirt.

The passage of the National Housing Act in 1934 signaled a new federal commitment to provide housing for the nation's citizens. Fifteen years later Congress made the commitment explicit in the Housing Act of 1949, establishing as a national goal the realization of "a decent home and suitable environment for every American family." To date, the commitment has not been consummated, and the resultant moral decay is not surprising. Indeed, "there are individual neighborhoods and areas within many cities where the housing situation continues to deteriorate." [5] Nor are these homes showplaces of properly healthful diet.

To remedy this blight on the American dream and its consequent impact on national obscenity rates, the Task Force recommends federal sponsorship, in whatever form and to whatever extent recommended by the Bureau of the Budget, of a program providing 600,000 low- and moderate-income housing units by next year, and 6 million units over the next five years. Supplementing such a program should be provisions for expanded and modified below-market interest rates, and a federal write-down of interest rates on loans to private builders. At the same time, urban renewal programs should be expanded and federal housing programs should be reoriented to place more low- and moderate-income housing outside of ghetto areas.

Such programs will, of course, be expensive, but even America cannot grow roses in a desert. There are simply no cheap ways to deal with a problem of this magnitude. We can detect the weed, and should extract it by the roots. In the words of former President Johnson,

> The only genuine, long-range solution for what has happened lies in an attack—at every level—upon the conditions that breed despair. . . . All of us know what those conditions are: ignorance, discrimination, slums, poverty, disease, not enough jobs. We should attack these conditions . . . because there is simply no other way to achieve a decent and orderly society in America.[6]

5. *Civil Disorders Report*, p. 467.
6. Address to the Nation, July 27, 1967.

Index